INSIDE
OUTSIDE

AN ACTION PLAN FOR
IMPROVING
THE PRIMARY SCHOOL ENVIRONMENT

Cherry Mares
Robert Stephenson

INSIDE OUTSIDE

was a contribution to
the European Year of the Environment,
by the
Tidy Britain Group Schools Research Project.

We would like to acknowledge the invaluable assistance given by teachers, advisers, local authorities, environmental projects and organisations and many others involved in environmental improvements of all kinds.

Inside Outside was written for Tidy Britain Group by the Tidy Britain Group Schools Research Project, Brighton Polytechnic.

© TIDY BRITAIN GROUP 1988

Reprinted 1992

ISBN 0 905277 09 0

Contents

Resources are at the end of each section, as appropriate.

CHAPTER 1.   Getting Started.

1.1 Introduction

A change for the better

Have you tried looking at your school, the classrooms, corridors and school grounds as if through the eyes of a visitor or one of the new first years?

How does it look? Stimulating? Inviting? Interesting? Or perhaps a bit drab, ordinary or even threatening? If you think there's room for improvement then this book is for you. It shows you how, by improving the inside and/or outside environment of your school - even a little - real benefits can follow.

Here are some proven benefits:
* a pleasanter place for work, play and recreation
* a valuable resource for all areas of the curriculum
* a means of developing positive and caring attitudes and behaviour
* improved relationships between pupils, teaching and non-teaching staff
* improved links with the wider community.

This has been the experience of a number of primary school teachers who have put ideas into practice and on which this book is based. They were not all blessed with smart schools to begin with, nor did they necessarily mount ambitious schemes. But they all improved their schools dramatically and experienced the benefits that anyone can share who tries out some of the ideas in this book.

Environmental improvement can be as simple as adding plants, pictures and carpets, or mounting displays in previously gloomy areas. Or at a more involved level, interior space can be replanned and corridors and classrooms can be reshaped. Some schools have been more ambitious and aimed at achieving coherence between the inside and the outside of the school, so that both classrooms and grounds are inviting and promise exciting learning and recreation. This message is part of the 'hidden' curriculum which is at least as important as the taught curriculum in influencing the attitude and behaviour of pupils towards each other, towards the school and their surroundings.

Improvement all round

The very process of improving the school can become an integral part of the taught curriculum and opens up many opportunities. Environmental improvement projects can involve pupils in learning new skills and concepts, in applying maths and science, humanities, language and design to real problems which have relevance to the pupils and which, in turn, can stimulate motivation and imagination.

In addition to the creation of a more pleasant environment and the provision of a curriculum resource, environmental improvement will often change behaviour patterns. Pupils involved in the planning and the care of a school improvement project will experience an increased sense of belonging which tends to counter irresponsible behaviour. Vandalism, litter and graffiti are all less likely and less tolerated in a school community where everyone is co-operating to create and sustain an enjoyable environment. Further, the confidence and self-respect that pupils gain from involvement with a project both as individuals and as members of a group are likely to contribute to their positive involvement in the wider community in later life.

Environmental improvement projects can also improve relationships between pupils and teaching and non-teaching staff and stimulate beneficial contact between the school and community. Parents and other adults may be involved in practical aspects and be influenced by their children's interest in environmental matters. Pupils may make contact with local industry and authorities and learn something of the constraints and decision-making processes of the adult world.

Finally, an environmentally enhanced school or school grounds will be enjoyed both by the pupils that created them and by the community, and stand as lasting proof of the value and power of group effort to achieve improvement for all.

Make the change!

From brightening up a corner to a thorough-going transformation of your school and grounds, the choice is yours. We hope this book will encourage and help you to start.

1.2 Planning a project

Whatever the idea to be carried out, the process of planning the scheme with the pupils is a vital and valuable educational experience. Careful planning is essential and success is more likely if certain stages and procedures are gone through and certain people involved.

The ideas described in the following pages range from small and traditional activities, through larger interior and exterior changes to fairly ambitious suggestions for landscaping and re-designing the school grounds. Unless all the teachers, pupils and the local education authority are committed and financial support is promised from the outset, it is advisable to start with a fairly simple and flexible plan which can be extended after initial success.

Suggestions for action

Involve teaching colleagues first, before the pupils. Discuss how the planning, execution and maintenance of a project can be used to enhance the curriculum and how the curriculum can be adapted to teach the skills which pupils will need in order to carry out the proposals. Ideally each proposal will be part of a long term and integrated curriculum development plan rather than something plucked from a shopping list of possible ideas. See Section 2.1.

Interest and involve the appropriate local authority officers. Contact the LEA advisory service and find out which of the advisers are interested in developing the school environment.

Inform and involve the PTA, governors and local community. It is best to do this at an early stage as they are invaluable sources of help and advice. It is essential to underline the educational value of the project (see Chapter 2) and to reassure parents that safety regulations will be followed at all times. See the case study 'Involving the community', on page 30.

Inform and involve the caretaker and non-teaching staff. Bring them into the project where possible as their co-operation is essential.

Form a steering/advisory group or committee. This should be a flexible grouping of PTA, governors, pupils, local community representatives, non-teaching staff and local authority officers. Continuity is more likely if it's a shared group effort and not dependent on individuals! See the case study 'Working with the committee' on page 7.

In areas where vandalism is a problem the involvement of pupils, parents and the community can be a protection, particularly if the amenity provided is for community use. In difficult areas it is as well to start changes in enclosed areas, in places which can be readily seen from nearby houses, or which are not easily accessible to passers-by. Try to replace damaged plants, trees or constructions as soon as possible.

Involve the pupils and ensure that they take part in all stages from the generation and selection of ideas to the final product. The pupils may well be introduced to the idea of improvement and change in an assembly, but some lesson time also needs to be devoted to discussing pupils' perception of the school, their likes and dislikes and suggestions for change. See 'Involving the pupils in selecting a project', page 5.

Interest and involve local independent groups and organisations likely to be of help. These may be architects and planners, community artists, local wildlife groups and other environmental and youth groups. Many pupils will belong to youth groups, some of which may well already hold meetings in the school. It may be possible to link youth and school work.

Produce a brief document outlining the proposed plans and resource needs. This should be done at an early stage and will be useful for fund and support raising and for explaining plans to people both inside and outside the school.

Keep the community informed. This can be done through exhibitions in and out of school, with items in the newsletter for parents, items on local radio, articles in local newspapers and appropriate parish or neighbourhood magazines. When publicising a successful event, take the opportunity to ask for any further help that is needed.

Take every opportunity to celebrate success and acknowledge individual and group achievements.

Planning, implementing and maintaining a project.

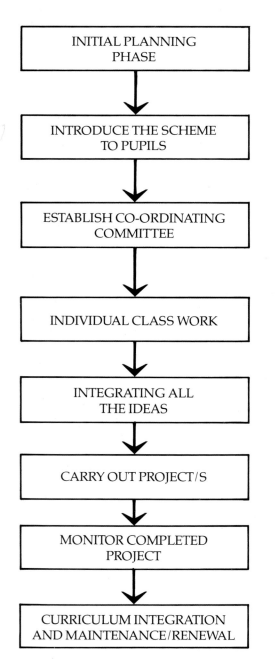

INITIAL PLANNING PHASE	encourage interest amongst all staff circulate **Inside Outside** discuss curriculum needs/possibilities with staff and advisers discuss improved play potential contact schools which have implemented environmental improvements contact outside help in local authority and voluntary sector collect other printed resources
INTRODUCE THE SCHEME TO PUPILS	at this stage only a planning exercise use assembly to inform whole school ensure pupils appreciate their active role and the value of scheme to them
ESTABLISH CO-ORDINATING COMMITTEE	flexible numbers and members to achieve objectives (not everyone need attend every meeting) key staff members non-teaching staff local authority representatives - planning/adviser/grounds parents voluntary bodies
INDIVIDUAL CLASS WORK	ideally whole site investigated but could divide amongst classes or start with smaller space, surveying, planning, measuring, model-making, library research, discussion, contacting council officers, preparing reports and much more
INTEGRATING ALL THE IDEAS	large exhibition for all plans draw together a final scheme if necessary break down into stages and create a sequence ensure all pupils will be involved seek project-specific funding/resources
CARRY OUT PROJECT/S	remember the importance of pupil involvement make the most of each step, develop parallel classroom work monitor and record changes
MONITOR COMPLETED PROJECT	monitor usage/development develop curriculum links - in-service provision, eg 'Baker Days' build on success in planning next phase assess pupil response
CURRICULUM INTEGRATION AND MAINTENANCE/RENEWAL	ideally maintenance will be curriculum-related, for example cutting a meadow gives seeds and compost some projects have finite life so that new ones can be planned to replace them, eg log-contained raised beds or murals.

Involving the pupils in selecting a project

Much of this work will inevitably take place within separate classes and all pupils should have the opportunity to be involved in overall site assessment and in discussing and understanding selection procedures. Subsequently, different classes could be allocated specific areas of the site or a competition could select the best overall scheme.

— Hold an initial brain-storming session, supported by maps and plans, (a large scale plan of the school and its grounds with a clear plastic 'wipe-off' overlay is useful). Follow this by direct experience with the pupils looking critically at the school and its grounds. Do not be tempted just to copy someone else's idea - what works for them may not work for you. Look closely at your site and develop its unique potential. Next consider each proposal in detail, break it down into steps and consider the requirements of time, skills and resources and the constraints imposed by the site. This can involve acquiring a variety of skills and information which might include, for example, identifying plants suitable for a shady corner, their costs and techniques of propagation, tracing the location of services underground before excavation, and finding the sources of the necessary materials. In this way realistic proposals will eventually be made.

— More time will be needed for the preparation, presentation and discussion of shortlisted proposals and for final negotiation and selection within the class. Ideally each class will arrive at a proposal which can be presented to the whole school, and to a committee of teachers, pupils, governors, PTA and interested outsiders. At this stage the mutually agreed school proposals should be in the form of detailed drawings and plans, with time scale, resources and the expert help required, and the likely outcomes and benefits, so that informed decisions can be taken.

— The process of final decision-making is also important. Unless all pupils recognise that one set of proposals is much the best there could be problems of maintaining interest, particularly if final choices do not incorporate something from each class. At this stage some collusion between staff may be necessary so that a compromise solution is selected which incorporates elements from all groups so that everyone is satisfied with the final decision.

Pupils can be encouraged to consider any changes as part of the long term development of the school and its grounds which will continue after they have gone. While planning the whole, they will have to recognise that they may be actively involved in the creation of only a relatively small part of it.

— Make sure that there is plenty of opportunity for pupils to be involved in a work programme and resist the temptation to use only a local MSC team to provide most of the labour for a large scheme. Modest projects carried out by the pupils create feelings of achievement and success whereas complex projects using mainly outside labour can leave pupils feeling that they are the outsiders.

– Once a decision has been taken and projects selected, the steering group can prepare a programme of work, plan the sequence of actions and timing, allocate tasks among groups or classes, select group leaders and identify the equipment, resources and expert help required.

Involving the community – Whitchurch Primary School, Avon.

Pupils, teachers, parents, CSV, YOP, the local secondary school craft and science workshops, the local authority Parks Department and Estates Services were among those involved in planning and implementing the first three years of a playground improvement scheme.

'The playground development started with a well thought out set of aims:

The product should — *improve the educational resources of the school*
— *improve the physical quality of the environment*

The process will — *involve pupils at all stages in the planning, design and creation of the scheme*
— *be linked to wider issues in the curriculum*

In October 1981, one hundred parents volunteered to assist and offered a wide range of skills and materials. In December 1981, sales of work raised £140.

The grounds were divided into potential project areas. Outside experts were brought in to work with class teachers and specific classes allocated areas of the grounds. For example the Avon Schools' Conservation Project worked with classes on projects including a tree nursery, drystone wall, butterfly reserve, small pond, bird table, nesting boxes and hedgerow creation.

Other bodies brought in (in addition to parents) included the Community Service Volunteers, Youth Opportunities Programme, local secondary school (science and craft workshop contacts), Parks Department (advice and materials) and County Estate Services (permissions and advice).

Other projects included:
* *yard paintings: maps of the Whitchurch area and of Great Britain, chess-board, compass, clock, school logo, number squares, spirals, alphabet game.*
* *outside wall battened for easy mounting of children's individual work.*
* *outside classroom/birdhide/weather station.*
* *outdoor seats and benches, play structures and plant containers.*

The whole programme was reinforced by newsletters, photo displays, noticeboards for ideas, visiting speakers and group meetings and reports.'

Mike Threlfall, Headmaster

Working with the committee - Gillespie Primary School, Islington, London N5.

'The involvement of the committee in the playstructure designs which were eventually realised in the school playground, illustrates the way things worked in practice.

At the beginning of the project an environmental steering committee was formed. The permanent members were: the deputy headteacher; two teachers each from the infant and junior departments; two women who were school helpers, dinner ladies and playground supervisors (one of whom was also a parent); a parent governor; a parent; eight child representatives of the four junior classes and Ms Teresa Boronska of the Islington Schools Environmental Project. The committee served as: a way of disseminating information - members reported back to the section of the school community they represented; a forum for discussing all the issues related to the environmental work going on in the school and as a decision-making body where necessary.

Islington Schools Environmental Project

Three classes of children worked on generating design ideas for new playstructures to be located in the playground. All the work they did was photographed and presented to the committee as an exhibition. This served as a focus for discussing all the issues involved - including health and safety, supervision, play potential, cost, location and its effect on essential services, present play arrangements and so forth. The children's work was discussed with reference to these issues and it was agreed that a selection of different design elements in the children's work should be developed to a final stage and precisely costed. The criteria used by the committee in selecting designs to be developed (play potential and structural integrity first having been agreed and confirmed) were, that they fell into different price bands - so that the committee could easily work to its budget for playstructures; that they were capable of combination with each other if possible - so the committee could have plenty of options and could design composite playstructures from the elements if necessary; and that they had different visual appearances - so the committee had a range of aesthetic options to choose from. The selected designs were subject to further work and represented to the committee with a detailed estimate of the cost of building each one. After three separate meetings of about an hour each, the committee decided on two different designs to be located separately. One was a modest low level structure from the lowest price band which it was felt might appeal to the younger pupils. The other was a much more substantial 'A' frame playstructure from the highest price band which the committee re-designed in two important respects. The overall height was reduced for health and safety reasons and one side of the frame was changed to incorporate a net, which was not in the children's original design, as it was felt that this would provide an alternative form of play and physical challenge. After checking that these designs fell within the budget and confirming with the inspectorate that they came within the health and safety guidelines the committee approved their construction.

One important effect of operating the committee was that it encouraged people to participate, and so issues of concern to certain sections of the school community were discussed. In relation to the playstructures, one small group of parents was particularly concerned about the safety aspects. The possibility of accidents and the context for these happening was extensively discussed, both to alleviate the justifiable concern of the parents and to help the committee in its role of designing for play. The success of the whole project as a participatory process was in part due to the effectiveness of the committee. As each environmental project evolved it was thoroughly discussed, relevant issues were raised and decisions taken in an open forum from which minutes were available.'

Islington Schools Environmental Project

Resources

Shell Better Britain Campaign information pack, free from
c/o British Trust for Conservation Volunteers
Red House
Red House Park
Hill Lane
Sandwell
West Midlands B43 6ND

In the London area:

Work to Play
Inter-Action
Royal Victoria Dock
London E16 1BT   Tel. 01-511 0411/6

*Work to Play aims to give children of 5 and over the experience of participating in the creation of their own environment. It provides a programme which includes drama, art work, modelling and design and gives the chidren the skills and confidence to design and, as much as is physically possible, create their own space. Consultation with teachers and parents is important, but **Work to Play** sees the work with children as the chief aim of any scheme.*

Free Form Arts Trust
(School Environment Improvements Project)
38 Dalston Lane
Hackney
London E8 3AZ   Tel. 01-249 3394

Islington Schools Environmental Project
Robert Blair School
Blundell Street
London N7 9BL   Tel. 01-700 4565

See also Resources 2.1.

1.3 Working with the Local Authority

With the exception of Inner London, education is the responsibility of County Councils or Metropolitan Boroughs in England, of County Councils in Wales and of Regional Councils in Scotland, though in all cases administration and servicing schools may be delegated to district level. For example, while the appropriate department of the District Council may maintain the school grounds and collect the rubbish, the roads within the school grounds may be maintained by the district highways department (acting as agent for the County) and both County and District Planning Departments may have an interest in any developments on the school site.

In practice, teachers and pupils can ask both authorities for assistance and many local authority departments have a very positive view of the role they can play in education and are happy to work in partnership with teachers. The naming of departments and the allocation of their responsibilities and functions vary from place to place, but the education department advisers will be able to give the necesary information.

Local authorities are increasingly supporting schools wishing to develop their grounds. Some have already identified individuals and working structures to help teachers to plan environmental improvements and obtain permission and advice. Others do not yet fully understand the potential educational value of environmental improvement projects and will require persistence on your part. Some authorities favour certain types or scale of project and it is as well to know this at an early stage. If your local authority is not yet enlightened, try to find contacts in local schools who have already tackled the problem and who may be able to help overcome obstacles.

It is essential to work within the framework of the local authority's various guidelines. The appropriate local authority staff should be informed and involved from the very beginning of any project where physical changes are likely to be made to the fabric of the school or in the school grounds. These include the Health and Safety Officer and (where the proposal makes it relevant) School Playing Fields Officer, Parks and Gardens Department, caretaker and cleaners and their local authority administrators. It is of prime importance from the outset to establish the demarcation lines of responsibility for the maintenance of particular areas and ensure that there are no later misunderstandings. For example in some authorities unless the correct liaison procedures are carried out via official channels, gang mowers will cut down developing meadows and tree seedlings and pesticides will be applied under hedges to suppress 'weeds' despite decisions taken by pupils, teachers and PTA that the area should become a wild garden.

Strict safety regulations have increased the duties of Health and Safety Officers and it is wise to call them in at an early stage. Other officers may be concerned to see that the proposals do not increase their workloads and in some cases negotiations may be necessary to change work schedules or working practices to allow the proposal to proceed.

The local authority can play a creative role in overcoming problems by providing advice, supplying resources, offering speakers and helping to publicise events. The enthusiasm of the response will depend on individuals and their past experience with schools. Once the project has been selected it will be helpful to invite the relevant officers to the school. Be prepared to illustrate your proposals with successful examples, possibly from this book.

It is worthwhile developing any personal contacts which already exist between members of staff and the local authority.

These departments may be useful (specific titles vary with different authorities):

County and District Planning Department

Advice on landscaping and design. The County Ecologist or Conservation Officer can be very helpful. Many planning departments already work closely with schools and will often be able to send a representative to join in discussion and even become a member of the team. They will be able to give information on practical matters such as services under the ground, liaise with surveyors and maintenance staff and may know other useful contacts. In some authorities they may even have access to small grants.

County and Town Engineer's and Highways Departments

Materials such as hardcore and broken paving slabs.

Parks and Recreation Department

Advice and training. Materials such as leafmould, plants, trees, soil, fenceposts and tree stakes.

Refuse Collection and Disposal Departments

Information on waste collection and disposal. (In England the district is responsible for waste collection and the county for disposal; it is different in Wales and Scotland.) The collection authority can often arrange for the refuse lorry to visit the school and for the team to meet the pupils. Disposal facilities can sometimes be visited or speakers arranged.

Environmental Health Department

(A district function.) Environmental Health Officers inspect shops, slaughterhouses and restaurants, deal with domestic health-related problems such as damp and noise and are responsible for the control of rodents and other pests. They may be able to provide speakers.

Resources

Teaching Resources for Environmental Education on School Sites

A guide produced jointly by the Education Department, the School Grounds Maintenance Service Unit of Devon County Council and some other educationalists. It shows how one county has arranged co-operation between departments to enable schools to make greater use of their grounds. Similar documents can be had from Surrey, West Sussex, Leicestershire, Hertfordshire, Hampshire, Kent and the London Boroughs of Enfield and Hounslow. Published by Devon Educational Television Service 1987
Widey Lane
Crownhill
Plymouth PL6 5JT   Tel. Plymouth 796379

1.4 Finding Tools and Materials

Tools and other equipment can probably be borrowed from parents or from the Parks and Gardens department.

Parents, local authorities and companies may find it easier to provide materials and lend tools than to donate money.

Local Conservation Volunteers often lend or supply tools at reasonable prices. Regional British Trust for Conservation Volunteers addresses are listed in Appendix 2. Affiliation to the BTCV brings insurance protection as well as guidance on the safe use of tools.

Once parents or local companies appreciate the purpose of the scheme, they may lend larger plant such as skips, a JCB, roller or lorry as appropriate.

Details of types of materials that may be required and their availability are listed in the appropriate sections.

1.5 Raising Money

Rewarding and worthwhile projects can be carried out without large amounts of money, so try to avoid the complications of proposals which need large scale external funding.

Funds are usually needed for materials and tools. Anything which can reduce the need to buy or hire should be tried before asking for money.

There are considerable educational and community benefits to be had by being resourceful and seeking out local cheap or free resources rather than applying for grants. The slower development of the project, the in-depth research and tenacity required can provide a more fruitful learning experience.

Before starting to look for sponsorship or help of any sort it is useful to have the aims and objectives of the project clearly and concisely documented, ideally on a single side of A4 paper. Outline the scheme, its educational and community value, estimates of time and materials required, costings and sources of labour. Where relevant, indicate working links with other professional bodies such as the Planning Department, or County Ecologist, and your own previous experience. It is also a good idea to list other assistance you have received and any other bodies you are approaching.

Match the aims of your project with those of the organisation you are approaching and then try to find the name of someone in the organisation who is likely to be sympathetic. If possible, arrange to visit them to explain your scheme personally. It is important to know exactly what you want and to have a clear idea of the ways the particular organisation can help. It is also useful to be able to offer them something in terms of publicity or improved relationship with the local community.

Two potentially helpful groups are the PTA and the local education authority. Then try local companies and explore any contacts between these and the PTA and Governors.

If you have an active PTA it will obviously already be raising funds from:
- jumble sales
- concerts
- sponsored events
- collecting and recycling materials (make sure you have a buyer)
- stalls (at local fairs or fêtes)
- sponsored litter pick-ups.

These events need considerable organisation and should not be embarked on lightly. It is best to find people with previous experience and to ensure that one person is responsible for planning the event.

Grants

Bodies providing grant aid include:
- county, town and borough councils
- local banks, insurance companies and building societies
- industrial and commercial companies
- trusts and foundations.

The following are particularly appropriate for environmental improvement projects:

Urban Aid Grants.
Details from the local authority.

Shell Better Britain Campaign Grants.
Information pack from address in Resources 1.2
(projects must include some aspect of community use).

Housing Action Area and General Improvement Area Grants.
Details from the district or borough council.

The Prince's Trust.
The Administrator,
Drapers' Hall,
London EC2N 2DQ.

Nature Conservancy Council School Conservation Area Grant.
Details from
NCC, Grants Section,
Northminster House,
Peterborough, PE1 1UA
(advisers have to support and countersign applications).

British Trust for Conservation Volunteers Groups offer assistance in finding grants. They know of national and local sources of money and can advise on the most profitable sources to try.

More details can be obtained from the 'Directory of Grant-Making Trusts' published by Charities Aid Foundation. Available in reference libraries. It is not easy to raise money from these trusts; success is more likely if you know someone who has a contact in the trust.

Useful publications on fundraising include:

Sources of Statutory Money: a guide for voluntary organisations.
Published by Bedford Square Press (1980) for the National Council of Voluntary Organisations.

Organise! - a guide to practical politics for youth and community groups
by Mark Smith for:
National Association of Youth Clubs,
Keswick House,
30 Peacock Lane,
Leicester LE1 5NY   Tel. 0533 29514.

Fundraising
A comprehensive handbook by Hilary Blume, published by Routledge & Kegan Paul.

ADVENTURE PLAYGROUNDS · ALLOTMENTS · BEACHES · BIRD SANCTUARIES · BOTTLE BANKS · CANALS AND TOWPATHS · CITY FARMS · COMMUNITY CENTRES · CONSERVATION AREAS DERELICT LAND · ELMS · ENERGY CONSERVATION · FENCES GRAFFITI · GRAVE YARDS · HERITAGE CENTRES · EMPTY HOUSES LAKES · LITTER · NATURE RESERVES · PAINTING · PICNIC SITES PONDS · PLAY AND RECREATIO *getting* SPORTS PITCHES · STONE CLE STREET FURNITURE · STATUES GREENS · WALLS · WASTE PAPER *help* WINDMILLS AND WATER MILLS · W *for community* PLANTING · VILLAGE GREENS · VI *environmental* PAPER · PLAYGROUNDS · ALLO *projects* SANCTUARIES · BOTTLE BANKS · FARMS · COMMUNITY CENTRES · CONSERVATION AREA · CYCLE WAYS · DERELICT LAND · ELMS · ENERGY CONSERVATION FENCES · GRAFFITI · GRAVE YARDS · HERITAGE CENTRES · EMPTY HOUSES · LAKES · LITTER · NATURE RESERVES · PAINTING PROJECTS · PONDS · PICNIC SITES · PLAY AND RECREATION FACILITIES · SHRUBBERIES · STONE CLEANING · BEACH LITTER BIRD SANCTUARIES · BOTTLE BANKS · CANALS AND TOWPATHS CITY FARMS · COMMUNITY CENTRES · DERELICT LAND · ELMS ENERGY CONSERVATION · GRAVE YARDS · HERITAGE CENTRES EMPTY HOUSES · LAKES · LITTER · NATURE RESERVES · PAINTING PROJECTS · PICNIC SITES · PLAY AND RECREATION FACILITIES SHRUBBERIES · SPORTS PITCHES · STONE CLEANING · STREAM CLEARANCE · LAKES · PAINTING PROJECTS · PONDS · PICNIC SHRUBBERIES · STONE CLEANING · ADVENTURE PLAYGROUNDS

SHELL BETTER BRITAIN CAMPAIGN

CHAPTER 2.
The benefits of environmental improvements

The ways that environmental improvements can benefit the whole school curriculum and community are discussed in this section. The potential benefits are of course interconnected and inseparable, but for the sake of clarity they are described separately under the headings - The Curriculum: Attitudes and behaviour: Play and development: Involving school support staff: Involving the community.

> **Coombes County Infant School, Arborfield, Berkshire, demonstrates how all aspects of school life can be enhanced by making more of the site.**
>
> 'The school grounds have been continuously developed since the school opened 15 years ago. It is established policy that new ways should be sought to increase the variety of environments in the school grounds. The intention is to make the outdoor environment as stimulating and rewarding as possible for play and learning. The children with the resident caretaker and other staff are involved in the creation and maintenance of the grounds. The community has been involved at all levels. Local residents offered materials and skills; parents, the army and other volunteers provided heavy labour for large tasks; local companies contributed materials and technical advice was given by departments of the local authority. Most importantly, the children have always been actively involved in the planning and creation of the features. Through this involvement they learn a caring attitude to the natural world and their school. During the year children raise chickens; grow, prepare and eat peas, beans, tomatoes and potatoes; grow sunflowers and spring bulbs; observe the development of amphibians; harvest a Christmas tree and study wildflowers and native trees in settings including woodland, coppice, ponds and marsh. All this plus play in such varied grounds and the regular addition to the grounds ensure that the project figures almost daily in the curriculum.'
>
> *Susan Humphries, Headteacher.*

2.1. The Curriculum

Planning and creating improvements to the school environment offers enormous opportunities for learning new skills, concepts and ideas in practical situations which have meaning and relevance for pupils.

Looked at in this context, even the planning and execution of apparently cosmetic changes such as making and planting window boxes can involve many skills. These include design, the use of tools, learning about growing media, propagation, the life cycle of plants, the selection of suitable species for a long flowering season and different exposures. Pupils may also develop an appreciation of colour and shapes and perhaps the beginning of a lifelong interest and pleasure in plants.

If small projects can offer so much, the possibilities of further enriching the curriculum through a development such as creating a pond are obvious. An integrated school policy of improving and exploiting the whole school environment and its grounds can substantially affect and revitalise the curriculum and increase opportunities for collaborative work between members of the teaching staff.

The planning process and the curriculum

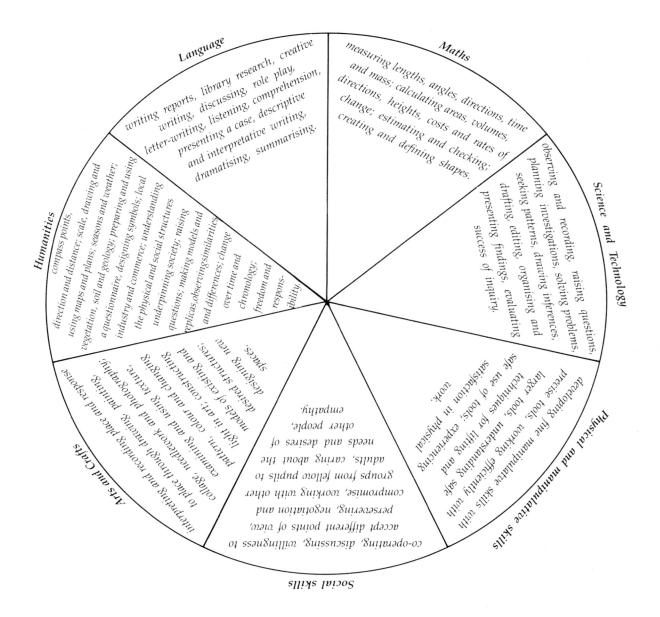

Language
writing reports, library research, creative writing, discussing, role play, letter-writing, listening, comprehension, presenting a case, descriptive and interpretative writing, dramatising, summarising.

Maths
measuring lengths, angles, directions, time and mass; calculating areas, volumes, directions, heights, costs and rates of change; estimating and checking; creating and defining shapes.

Science and Technology
observing and recording, raising questions, planning investigations, solving problems, seeking patterns, drawing inferences, drafting, editing, organising and presenting findings, evaluating success of inquiry.

Physical and manipulative skills
developing fine manipulative skills with precise tools; working efficiently with larger tools; understanding and techniques for lifting; experiencing safe use of tools; satisfaction in physical work.

Social skills
co-operating, discussing, willingness to accept different points of view, persevering, negotiation and compromise, working with other groups from fellow pupils to adults, caring about the needs and desires of other people, empathy.

Arts and Crafts
interpreting and recording place and response to place through drawing, painting, collage, needlework and photography, examining, colour and changing texture, light in art, constructing and pattern, using and constructing models of existing and designing spaces.

Humanities
compass points, direction and distance; scale, drawing and using maps and plans; seasons and weather; vegetation, soil and geology; preparing and using a questionnaire, designing symbols; local industry and commerce; understanding the physical and social structures underpinning society; raising questions; making models and replicas, observing similarities and differences; change over time and chronology; freedom and responsibility.

15

Suggestions for action

Identify one teacher as a curriculum leader. If there is already a teacher with special responsibility for curriculum development or environmental education, this is likely to be the appropriate person. If not, a teacher should be found to co-ordinate the curricular aspects of the work.

Hold a meeting for all staff members to discuss their immediate and long term curriculum and resource needs. Relate these to the project proposals being considered.

The lists of skills, concepts, experiences and content appropriate to the core curriculum subjects should be available for this meeting. Teachers will be reassured to realise that a project involving pupils in planning, implementing, using and maintaining any form of environmental improvement in the school or its grounds can, quite naturally, involve the range of items listed in the core curriculum guidelines provided by the DES, and various subject associations.

It is useful to ask each subject specialist to consider ways their particular curriculum demands could be met through the proposed project. This process need not be overwhelming. For example, consider how you might work with a class on studying the grounds with a view of creating more varied resources for work and play. Such a project could greatly assist the attainment of the curriculum objectives shown below.

'The curriculum for the early years should provide pupils with learning experiences of a geographical nature that will enable them to

- extend their awareness of, and develop their interest in, their surroundings
- observe accurately and develop simple skills of inquiry
- investigate at first-hand features of their local environment: its weather; its surface features; and some of the activities of its inhabitants, especially those aspects that involve spatial and environmental relationships
- have some understanding of changes taking place in their own locality … including some appreciation of the ways in which human decisions influence these changes
- gain some appreciation of the importance of location in human affairs and understand some of the ways in which the local environment affects people's lives
- distinguish between the variety of ways in which land is used and the variety of purposes for which buildings are constructed
- develop an awareness of seasonal changes of weather and of the effects which weather conditions have on the growth of plants, on the lives of animals and on their own and other people's activities
- gain some understanding of the different contributions which a variety of individuals and services make to the life of the local community
- begin to develop an interest in people and places beyond their immediate experience
- become acquainted with a variety of maps, including large scale maps of their own neighbourhood, and be able to apply simple techniques of map reading and interpretation
- appreciate the significance of people's attitudes and values in the context of particular environmental or social issues which they have investigated.'

Curriculum Matters. Geography 5 - 16.
HMI Series. See Resources 2.1.

In a similar way it is not difficult to see how a pond, woodland edge or wet ditch could be used to teach the following science concepts.

'Living things depend on each other in various ways.

Some animals eat plants and some eat other animals, but all animals ultimately depend on green plants for food.

Living things are usually well-suited in form and function to the environment in which they are found.

Air fills the space around or near the earth's surface.

Water is essential to life. It makes up a large proportion of all living things.

Soil, a mixture of things, comes from rocks and living things.

Plants take substances from both the air and the soil.

Substances taken from the soil must be replaced to maintain fertility.

Changes in the physical environment due to seasonal cycles are often matched by changes or events in the living world, such as fruiting or mating.

Air contains water vapour which condenses in various conditions.

There are many different plants and animals which between them show a variety of ways of carrying out life processes.

All living things need food for growth and repair as well as for reproduction and movement.

Green plants can make food, animals cannot.

All living things produce waste materials in carrying out life processes.

Most living things take in oxygen from the air or from the water in which they live.

Living things produce offspring of the same "species" as themselves.

The life cycle of any living thing is repeated in each generation.

All living organisms have means of receiving information from their environment.

Water tends to flow until its surface reaches a common level.

Objects completely immersed in a liquid displace a volume of liquid equal to their own volume.

Some substances float in water, others sink unless they are made into objects having a hollow shape.

The apparent movements of the sun, moon and stars follow a regular pattern.'

From the APU Science Progress Report, see Resources 2.1.

Decide what use each class and age group will make of the new resources. This should be done as soon as a plan has been proposed and accepted by pupils, PTA, teachers and governors. Try to avoid unnecessary repetition and duplication and ensure progression of skills/concept development.

Make the most of every opportunity for learning monitoring and survey skills and ensure that detailed records of all kinds are kept from the outset, preferably by the children.

Many of the skills needed to survey and record can be taught in formal lessons and the experience is a good incentive for learning graphs, measurement of area and volume, averages and statistical sampling, percentages, sets and group theory, pie charts and histograms.

Record decisions: plans, progress of work, material used, costs, change and growth over several years.

Use reports, maps, surveys, drawings, poems, models, descriptive writing, drama, and film as contributions to a data base.

Try to keep an up-to-date diary/scrap book of examples of work, photographs, drawings, etc.

Make sure the parents and governors understand and appreciate the educational value to be derived from planning the project, particularly that:

– Subjects such as maths, science and skills such as reading, writing and spelling (of major concern to most parents) will be enhanced rather than neglected by the planning and implementation of the project. An ongoing display of plans, feasibility studies, reports, records and photographs will all help in the reassuring process. Should parents and governors need more detailed information about the contribution environmental improvement projects can make to the achievement of curriculum objectives, the information on page 16 may be of use.

– The project will help develop communication, presentation, negotiation, decision-making and interpersonal skills. It will bring relevance to much of the curriculum and provide a valuable resource for learning traditional subjects.

– The process of investigation and consultation, the formulation of proposals, further consultation and revision and the preparation and implementation of a plan of work is a valuable learning experience which applies to a variety of situations in adult life.

– The project provides contact with, and understanding of, the local authority committees, officers and services. It can also offer contact with industry and commerce and some understanding of the complex system of permissions, rules and regulations which are part of any development.

– The project will encourage positive caring and responsible attitudes and behaviour.

– According to the nature of the proposed improvement, it may also provide added resources for the development of physical skills, play and recreation.

Plan some developments so that new pupils will become involved. It is the early planning and creation that help children to develop positive attitudes to their environment:

- seasonal crop areas and tree nursery
- constructions which gradually decay such as raised beds retained by logs which will need regular renewal
- willow beds for harvesting canes for basketry
- murals which can be replaced annually
- hanging baskets and window boxes of annuals
- corridor displays and exhibition areas.

Incorporate maintenance into the curriculum. The process of maintaining green schemes (ponds, meadows, woods, etc) demonstrates clearly that all 'natural' environments in this country are created or managed by man and that without this influence all vegetation moves through a predictable sequence of changes towards a climax:

- cutting the meadow becomes seed collection, composting and biomass production calculation
- painting furniture leads to a study of protective coatings
- raking up leaves becomes an opportunity for leaf study, artwork and printing as well as an excuse for a bonfire.

Look for ways to extend projects beyond the obvious

- A group of schools in Oxfordshire extend vegetable growing into marketing, profit and loss, bookkeeping and so to raising money to support school garden projects in Thailand. Twinned schools exchange cassettes, artwork and stories about lifestyles, favourite foods, festivals, etc.
- A school tree nursery in Birmingham has a linked mini-company to market its products and to develop links into the local community.

Remember that curriculum resources do not have to be living. School grounds can be used for all kinds of areas of the curriculum from sculpture corners to history projects as in this example:

'The Iron Age has come to life for pupils at Cranborne Middle School in Dorset.

Cranborne's Iron Age hut was designed by fourth-year pupils (12 and 13 year olds). It is based partly on a reconstructed Iron Age farm at Butser in Hampshire seen by the pupils, and partly on the archaeological evidence of post holes. The children also worked out that the roof would have to slope at an angle of 45 degrees to stop the rain getting in.

Work started in April 1985, when pupils and parents cut wood for the hut. More than a hundred eager volunteers then helped to dig the four-foot ditch which enclosed the settlement and kept out animals.

Roof rafters had to be fixed to the main posts and wattle walls constructed, with help from a parent who is a hurdle-maker. A group of 9 and 10 year-olds made the ring beams which go round the rafters and hoisted them on.

The £500 grant from the SCDC all went on reeds for the roof thatch.

A professional thatcher spent a day at the school teaching pupils how to thatch and came away most impressed with the thatching skills of the 12 year-olds. The children used authentic tools, biddles, which they had made themselves, to push the reeds tightly together over the wooden framework.

Then came daubing day, plastering the wattle with daub made from mud, straw and manure, which turned into an open-air festival with pupils, parents and friends from the village all lending a hand. "It took three days to get the smell of the daub off my hands," one 12 year-old girl said with delight.

Future plans include building a Roman kiln to fire pupils' pottery, bronze-casting and flint-knapping - shaping flint tools with authentic tools. The settlement and hut will provide extra room for drama and natural history lessons; the hut has already been colonized by wrens, pheasants, insects and mice.

Weaving may be on the syllabus, too. Pupils will make looms in CDT lessons and extract nettle fibres for weaving.

Mr Keen believes pupils have already gained valuable problem-solving skills from the project, as well as new practical abilities.

The children themselves say they have enjoyed learning about the Iron Age through building the settlement. "I used to think history was really boring, but in the Iron Age people had a lot of adventures - hunting, growing their own crops. Their life was full of challenges," said 12 year-old Sandra Wills. "It's much more interesting than listening to stories about Romans fighting."

"Making the hut was much better than reading about it in a classroom. You learn more by doing things," explained 11 year-old Nigel Friend. And others said they liked having a teacher who could teach about two different things.'

Adapted from 'Invent your Tools, then Build a Hut',
Times Educational Supplement
14 March 1986.

Resources

Environmental Education in the Primary School
One of a range of resource lists priced between 10p and 40p, sae with enquiries to
Council for Environmental Education (CEE)
University of Reading
London Road
Reading RG1 5AQ

Geography from 5 to 16
DES, HMI Series Curriculum Matters 7. HMSO 1986
ISBN 01 270606

History in the Primary and Secondary Years - an HMI View
DES, HMSO 1985

Assessment of Performance Unit Science Progress Report 1977-8
List of Science Concepts and Knowledge
Assessment of Performance Unit
Department of Education and Science
Elizabeth House
York Road
London SE1

Teaching Children through the Environment
Pamela Mays, Hodder and Stoughton 1985

Urban Studies Centres
Report by HM Inspectors, 1985
Department of Education and Science (address above)

Making the Most of your School Grounds (parts 1 and 2)
by Gill Thomas   £5 inc. p&p each
Very useful bound sheets on planning, liaison with local authority departments and the creation
and subsequent use of selected features (eg butterfly garden, pond, play areas and structures),
many starting points for cross-curricular studies are described.
Science Teacher Advisory Resource Team (START)
Mayhill Junior School
The Bury
Odiham
Basingstoke
Hants   Tel. (025 671) 3766

Starting a School Garden
David Gale   £2.95 + £1.50 p&p
School Garden Company
PO Box 49
Spalding
Lincs. PE11 1NZ

Planning your School Nature Garden
Urban Spaces Scheme
Polytechnic of North London
Holloway Road
London N7 8DB   £3.50 inc. p&p

Planting Whips and Teaching from Treeplanting
Plants of Walls and Pavements
Ladybirds
Spiders
and more from the
Urban Spaces Scheme, details from above address.

Come Outside

£25 + £1.50 p&p VHS video tape showing the remarkable range of projects tackled in Coombe County Infant School, Arborfield, Berks.
Bob Bray
54 Crofton Road
Camberwell
London SE5 8NB

Grounds for Conservation

£2 inc. p&p
Hertfordshire County Council
County Hall
Hertford SG13 8DF

Video cassettes on the natural environment and its conservation

Information Sheet No 10
Information and Library Services
Nature Conservancy Council
Northminster House
Peterborough PE1 1UA

Lancashire looks at ... Science in the Early Years

by Lancashire County Council, 1986.
Produced by teachers for use with younger pupils (up to 8 years), it contains many useful case studies and curriculum outlines which could be the basis for work using developments in the school grounds including minibeasts, weather, birds, school nature trail, growing things and caring for plants.
Contact Education Resources Unit, for price and availability at
County Hall
Fishergate
Preston, Lancs. PR1 8RJ   Tel. (0772) 54868

The Tree Games Pack

A collection of games to make learning about trees more fun.
The Environment Centre
Drummond High School
Cochran Terrace
Edinburgh EH7 4QP   Tel. (031) 557 2135

Sharing Nature with Children

by Joseph Cornell
Contains many useful games and ideas for their expansion to introduce basic ecological concepts to young children. Obtainable from
Exley Publications Ltd
16 Chalk Hill
Watford WD1 4BN   Tel. (0923) 50505

Environmental Education: guidelines for the Primary and Middle Years

A very useful document to help fix the scope and set objectives for curriculum planning.
Hertfordshire County Council
County Hall
Hertford SG13 8DF

Using the Environment

A series of six volumes in the 'Series in Science 5/13 Project', brim-full of ideas and techniques for developing and using the school's outdoor environment.
1. Early Exploration
2. Investigations, Part 1
3. Tackling problems, Part 1
*   Part 2*
4. Ways and means.
Published for the Schools Council by Macdonald 1974 - 77.

Small Wonder *and a selection of extra packs* (**Introduction to Ecology, Gardening for Wildlife, Woodlands, Hedgerow History and Ecology, Freshwater Life, and others**)
Main pack is £12.95 and contains photocopyable sheets on lifecycles of many common small animals, information on ants, bees and spiders, life in compost logs, flower pollination. Throughout the text there are many ideas for practical projects that pupils can set up and study. A fascinating resource pack which will ensure that the curriculum links are quickly established.
by Mari Friend,
Bug Box Optix
FREEPOST (BR 321)
Hove
E Sussex BN3 2ZZ

A place to live in together *and* **Hedgerows information pack** *two of the useful resources from the RSPCA. Send s.a.e. for full list and prices.*
RSPCA
Causeway
Horsham
W Sussex RH12 1HG

Teaching Resources for Environmental Education on School Sites (TREES)
and also **Chequerboard Gardens, Tree Nurseries, Studies in Freshwater Life, Studying Minibeasts** *and* **Study Birds** *from*
Devon Educational Television Service
Widey Lane
Crownhill
Plymouth   Tel. (0752) 796379

2.2 Attitudes and behaviour

Being involved in the process of planning, creating and maintaining an environmental improvement can have a marked effect on children's attitudes to school, to themselves, to other people and to their surroundings.

It may well be the first time that some children enjoy school and look forward to getting on with what they are doing there. It may also be their first taste of the pleasures of handling wood and stone, of growing things, and of caring for plants and animals - all satisfying and fulfilling experiences which encourage maturity and a sense of ownership and, through joint endeavour, of belonging to the class, school and community. Children also appreciate the shared responsibility in working with adults rather than for them and being trusted with work which will have a greater and longer lasting impact than drawing or writing on a sheet of paper.

Environmental improvements demand a variety of skills and qualities which are not always in evidence in traditional classroom work. Some children experience both a sense of personal achievement and group acceptance for the first time when their previously unrecognised abilities and ideas are appreciated.

It is most important that children should value the work they are doing and see it as worthwhile, rather than as just paying lip-service to involving them in improving the school environment. In Sweden all schools are obliged to give pupils *'increased responsibility and powers of influence in line with their increasing maturity and age'*. Teachers do not always find this easy and research at the Dept. of Educational Research of Stockholm Institute of Education found that in many schools responsibility was reduced to a rota for chores like airing the classroom, 'head of table' at lunchtime and helping the school caretaker. Pupils saw these roles as junior or subservient and, in the case of 'tidying up after the class' pointless, *('If they could hang up their coats and put their shoes together we wouldn't have to do it',).* Two jobs consistently seen as rewarding and worthwhile were looking after the aquaria and watering the plants; purposeful activities which are much more aligned to the philosophy of 'Inside Outside.'

It is the involvement with long term more permanent improvements that is likely to bring most satisfaction, while the maintenance of these projects brings a sense of continuity and responsibility. Even young children are well aware of the value of the changes to which they have contributed. Not only do they appreciate the importance themselves, but they want others to do the same and they are prepared to put continuing effort into caring for the environment they have created. They will also try to think of ways to protect the new environment and prevent it being damaged or vandalised.

Many teachers have commented on improved behaviour and of a general reduction in litter, graffiti and vandalism.

'It does work. I wouldn't have believed it before I took this job but involving kids in creating areas does stop vandalism. And, I don't understand how, but it seems to spread from directly involved children to others.'

Keith Williams
Wigan Groundwork Trust

and –

'Since the playground has been redeveloped the children show more interest and care for their school. After holidays many go around the garden looking for the changes that have taken place. Many have bought plants and packets of seeds with their pocket money. There is concern if any pot plants are accidentally broken. New children are quickly told by the older pupils: "We look after our school".'

Sister Lorna, Headteacher
St Mary's School, Erskineville,
Sydney, Australia.
From 'The Story of a Playground' by Anne Kern
Published Artchitecture Australia 68, 1979

Teachers who have been involved in environmental improvements emphasise the importance of children learning that they can have influence over the form and quality of their environment.

'Environmental projects are extremely important. If children are made aware at an early age that they are the creators of their own environment then perhaps they will make conscious efforts in their daily lives to maintain pleasant and attractive surroundings in which to live and work.'

Helena King,
St Philomena's Primary School, Glasgow.

Environmental work can help to change the nature of a group and encourage real co-operative effort. Teachers have noticed that, when working towards a practical outcome, groups tend to become less aggressive and competitive than when a more 'academic' outcome is expected.

Certainly environmental improvement projects can help to change pupils' attitudes towards members of staff - and vice versa. Pupils who are frequently disruptive or withdrawn in class can become more open, friendly and co-operative when enjoying creating a new environment. Teachers who are preoccupied with work and discipline may become more relaxed and show another side of their natures - to everyone's benefit.

Recognition of the validity of an emotional response to place is an important aspect of education; it is often undervalued yet it is a crucial factor in being able to come to terms with many issues in daily life. One element of the process of involving children in improving the school environment is to encourage them to recognise and analyse their feelings towards the school and its grounds and to treat such response as valuable. To learn that dislike and frustration are as acceptable responses as pleasure and delight, and that both sets of emotions can be channelled into action is a healthy and constructive process which can lead to improved personal relationships as well as an improved environment.

2.3 Play and development

Many ideas for improving the school environment relate to play. It has been estimated that approximately 30% of most primary children's time at school is spent in either formal or informal play in the school grounds. Inevitably the quality of the experience has considerable influence on a child's attitude to school and shapes personal and social development and behaviour. Research into playspace and behaviour suggests that increasing the variety of forms, spaces and structures leads to a reduction in disruption through a reduction in boredom. Small intimate playspace is often necessary for fantasy and imagination games; pupils do not always want to rush about and the opportunity for quiet reflection or sitting in the sun is important. Satisfying play in grounds where there are opportunities for many different kinds of play to occur simultaneously is also thought to minimise bullying and accidents, and there is a strong connection between playground experiences and the ability to settle down and concentrate when returning to the classroom.

Coombes County Infant School

Recent publications on play reinforce the need for variety:

'... the need for thoughtful design and the introduction of a variety of equipment, materials and space to create playground environments providing balanced opportunities for play. Play theory suggests that some types of play behaviors are more desirable than others for their contribution to socialization and cognitive development. If this premise is accepted, then the creative playground scoring higher for associative, co-operative, constructive and dramatic play would appear to provide more opportunity for development.'

'The effects of playground type on the cognitive and social play behaviors of grade two children' Sheila D Campbell and Joe L Frost in 'When Children Play', pub. Association for Childhood Education International 1985, U.S.A.

'Research has also indicated that the physical and social environments directly influence a child's development and that a stimulating, rich, and varied environment is essential in enabling the child to reach his or her greatest potential. The growing child is developing characteristics that are most susceptible to environmental influence, so it is vital that any setting designed for children's use - whether a day-care center, schoolroom, or playground - provide as much stimulation as possible.'

from 'Playground Design' by Aase Eriksen, pub. Van Nostrand Reinhold, New York. 1985.

Suggestions for action

Consider the wide variety of different possibilities for play structures and facilities in relation to the particular environment of your school and the needs of your pupils.

See especially sections 1.2 and 3.2.1.

A long term project carried out with the Newcastle Architecture Workshop to develop playground plans with pupils in Lemington First School, Newcastle, see Resources 2.3.

The project aims to improve the facilities of the school playground so that the whole of the educational premises becomes a resource for learning and developmental play. Pupils surveyed the school, using the BBC micro-computer and the Turtle programme to draw the plan. Some of the ways they had worked out levels were by counting the bricks along the caretaker's house wall, and also by using tanks of water and measuring the effect of putting them on a slope. They made models and produced imaginative drawings of how they would like their playground to look and explained their ideas to each other. Finally their ideas were turned into workable designs by the architects and erected by a Community Programme team. Continued interest in the development will be encouraged by allowing for changes - furnishing and decorating the house dens, painting new murals, adding a ceramic mural, growing plants and observing insect life.

JACK AND THE BEANSTALK

store

flower bed

store

caretakers house

Mr Percival's car desire line.

Surface Game based on Jack and the Beanstalk by School

LOGS 350mm high

LOGS 700/750mm high

LOGS

Hen

Daisy

LOGS 200mm high

Jack's mothers Cottage

safety surface

Giants Castle

Golden Eggs / mosiac by School

Leapfrog Poles

Beanstalk Poles

LOGS

desire line

garden

desire lines

Giant's Boots by School

girls toilets

wall painting of Giant by School

main school building

LEMINGTON FIRST SCHOOL ADVENTURE PLAYGROUND

PLAN   scale 1:100

1.2m safety zone around play equipment.

Newcastle Architecture Workshop Ltd.

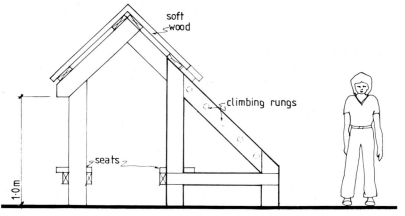

soft wood

climbing rungs

seats

1·0 m

FRONT ELEVATION (south)

LEMINGTON FIRST SCHOOL ADVENTURE PLAYGROUND

JACK'S MOTHERS COTTAGE for climbing, sitting.

Newcastle Architecture Workshop Ltd.

Provide a storage space for play equipment. This could be a small shed or ex-storeroom where equipment such as mats, skipping ropes and balls could be kept, as well as boxes, tyres, benches for building. The playstore can be looked after by different classes in turn who would loan equipment and supervise storage, etc.

Provide opportunities for children to choose to join in constructively supervised play. Parents, ancillary staff and other members of the community and older children may be willing to organise traditional ball, skipping or round games, or country dancing, on one or more playtimes a week.

Resources

Playground Design: outdoor environments for learning and development
Aase Eriksen
Van Nostrand Reinhold, New York, 1985

Lemington Playground Design
Newcastle Architecture Workshop
6 Higham Place
Newcastle upon Tyne NE1 8AF   Tel. (091) 2328183

2.4. Involving school support staff

Finding out about the work of the many different individuals working in the school helps children to understand how the school functions and how they can contribute to its smooth running. The following suggestions are in addition to the much closer relationship which will develop as projects are planned.

Suggestions for action

Each class could find out about the work of different members of the school support staff, such as cleaners, caretakers and dinner helpers. A study of the school cleaners could include how far they travel to work, how long the journey takes, who organises their working day, how it is spent, and the proportion of time given to sweeping, dusting and floor cleaning compared with less frequent jobs such as cleaning walls and blinds. Staff could be asked about the particular satisfactions and frustrations of their work and for suggestions on improving the appearance and smooth running of the school. The work of the secretarial, ancillary staff, caretakers and people who work in the school grounds may be examined in the same way.

The children could also find out about the work of the teaching staff. How much time is spent on preparing lessons, marking, record keeping, PTA and staff meetings, rehearsals, team visits, etc? What do teachers do at playtime in the staffroom? How do they spend their leisure?

The children could draw up a list of proposals for making work easier and pleasanter for both teaching and non-teaching staff. In fairness, children should also be asked what the staff can do to make the children's lives pleasanter. Improved relationships and increased efficiency can result from regular frank exchanges of ideas between children and adults.

Discuss, list and photograph all the people who come to work in the school at various times, find out the frequency of their visits and what they do. These could include the school nurse, dentist and other health staff, meter readers, refuse collectors, oil, coal and milk delivery personnel as well as rarer callers such as decorators, builders, glaziers and photographers.

Mrs Kureshi is putting the rubbish in a sack. Her little boy helps her   Tracey

Mrs Johnson is mopping the art corner floor   Marcia

Mrs Champany is sweeping the floor   Narinder

PUPILS' PAINTINGS OF THE SCHOOL CLEANERS

Resources

Look Around the Town - First Steps in Understanding the Urban Environment
Our Environment

See Tidy Britain Group materials, Appendix 1.

Both the above publications give more suggestions for projects involving the teaching and non-teaching staff of the school.

2.5 Involving the community

Many environmental improvement projects will need help and resources from outside the school. This should not be seen as a stumbling block, but rather an opportunity to bring the children and the wider community together to their mutual benefit. Parents and other adults who have been involved with environmental improvement projects in their local school have commented on their own change of attitude and increased concern and understanding of environmental matters. Contacts made for a specific project may grow into valuable links with, say, local companies or community associations.

CREATING A COMMUNITY GARDEN

Suggestions for action

Parents and other adults could be asked to accompany pupils on visits, to supervise small working groups in the school grounds, to talk about their work and to help pupils with practical environmental acitivities such as improving the school grounds, organising a recycling scheme, clearing up a local beauty spot or running an environmental club. Parents can also give valuable support if the school is taking part in one of the many environmental award schemes such as the Shell Better Britain Campaign. (See Resources 1.2.)

An exhibition of pupils' work in the school, local library, civic or community centre is a good way of reaching the local community. Exhibitions can be organised in conjunction with the Tidy Britain Group, with local litter abatement campaigns or environmental improvement projects, or in their own right. Working towards exhibitions and competitions gives many children additional motivation.

School governors have an increasing role to play in the life of the school and like to be informed of particularly interesting projects. Governors frequently know the local community well and may provide useful contacts, facilitate visits or arrange speakers.

The Chamber of Commerce, Rotary Club or local industries may well be interested in activities such as the various surveys or environmental improvement projects which might involve their members. They may be able to provide speakers, arrange visits or find resources.

Various departments of the local authority (borough, district and county) are likely to be rich sources of support. While contact with the various departments might eventually lead to an improvement in local facilities, it is also useful for pupils to understand the role and influence of the local authorities. Information on the structure of local government is readily available from local authority offices.

Local press and radio are always on the look out for interesting items and provide publicity which serves the valuable function of helping children appreciate that their work is of importance and interest to the adult world.

Pupils carrying out surveys on facilities, resources, pollution or the quality of the local environment can discuss their findings with local people. Where appropriate this information can be passed to the local authorities or other agencies for action, thus providing a model for active participation in local affairs.

The school, working with the PTA and governors, can make a policy decision to be involved with nearby community bodies such as the community association, physically handicapped group, playgroup, community garden project and old people's home committee.

CUTTING STEPS IN A STEEP SLOPE

Local people and a school adopted this steep piece of land, cleared dumped refuse, fenced it, created gardens along the level top section, put in walks including paths and steps on the hillside and created a pond in the wetter bottom section. What had been an area to avoid became one to cherish.

Resources

Once the nature of the community involvement becomes clear, the earlier resource lists for more specific types of project will be useful.

Rotary Club
Lions' Club
Community and Residents' Associations *Enquire at the local reference library.*
The local Chamber of Commerce

Local secondary schools
Schools Curriculum Industry Project (SCIP)
Industry Education Liaison (INDEL) officers

can be contacted via the
education department.

Local radio and newspapers
and other local companies, groups and organisations.

Vandalism
tape/slide sequence produced on a Leeds housing estate. Involves pupils from a nearby school and affected residents. Useful discussion starter.
£14 + VAT,
The Slide Centre Ltd
Ilton
Ilminster
Somerset TA19 9HS   Tel. (0460) 57151

Shell Better Britain Campaign, *see Resources 1.2*

CHAPTER 3: Making Improvements

3.1   Inside

3.1.1 Classrooms

We have all seen well organised, welcoming and interesting classrooms in the same building as ones that are bleak and shabby. Despite undoubtedly severe constraints, it is still possible to improve bleak classrooms and give children a sense of pride in their surroundings.

In the ideal classroom

* pupils feel safe, valued and accepted
* individual pupils have their own 'base' where their possessions can be safely kept
* there are plenty of books and a comfortable place in which to sit and read
* there are interesting things to look at and to do in spare time
* there is time and space for both children and adults to talk
* there are well tended living things
* displays of work are well presented and frequently changed
* equipment is well maintained, neatly stored and accessible.

However pleasant the existing classroom may be, once the children become involved in a whole school policy of environmental education and improvement, they are likely to question a variety of assumptions, to look at their classroom with new eyes and to have ideas which they will want to discuss and implement. These may be wildly expensive and utopian and need major building works, or they may be strictly practical and possible. All ideas should be seriously discussed and implemented whenever possible and where this is not possible, pupils should understand the problems and limitations.

Many of the ideas will concern the physical environment, but there will also be the opportunity to discuss the social environment and the individual's need to feel secure and valued while accepting responsibility for other people within the class and school community.

Suggestions for action

Lay a carpet to reduce noise and increase comfort. It need not be expensive and is well worth any effort involved in raising money. Thin rubber-backed carpets are easily cleaned and can be laid selectively, avoiding potentially dirty working areas.

Put cushions on a carpeted floor to encourage quiet reading. If space is no problem, designate and screen off part of the room for reading in comfort in junior as well as infant classes.

Consider lowering the ceiling if classrooms are high and echoing. This will improve acoustics, reduce noise and save energy. Few authorities will have money available for minor work programmes and this may well involve fund-raising or local sponsorship.

Make the most of the local art gallery loans service. If this doesn't exist, persuade the gallery directors to lend pictures and involve the children in selecting and hanging them.

Set aside some time each term/month for repairing books. Once the pupils know what they are doing, keep the materials readily available as a wet-playtime or spare-time activity. Make a list of books that have been repaired and by whom, and allow the children to put their names inside the back cover of books they have repaired.

Repairing library books is a good practical example of reuse and of conserving resources and saving money while at the same time giving motivation for looking after books that have already been mended. It could also lead to interest in bookbinding and projects on printing, illustrated manuscripts, publishing, etc.

Improve storage. Pictures, sets of small books, maths and science equipment can often be made more accessible and so more readily used. Containers can be made from cardboard boxes cut down, covered with wallpaper or fabric as available, and labelled.

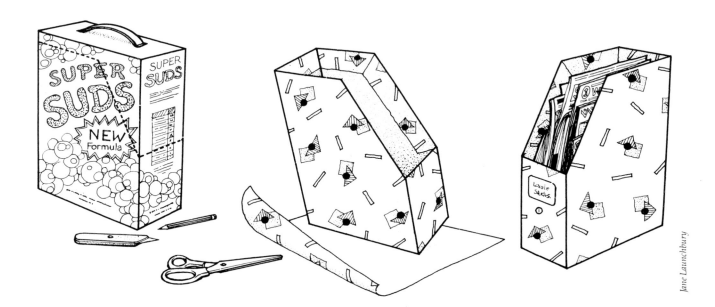

Jane Launchbury

35

Resources

Bookbinding as a Handcraft
by Manly Banister, pub. Sterling, New York, distributed in UK by Blandford 1986. Includes some simple techniques.

3.1.2 Corridors and cloakrooms

Corridors and cloakrooms can be lively, colourful and interesting places but they are generally without character and may be the target for vandalism. If pupils are personally involved in the quality of the space, they can gain real satisfaction from any improvements they have initiated. They are also more likely to behave responsibly in places where they have been responsible for design, decoration and upkeep. Caretakers and cleaning staff should be consulted before changing the position of heavy furniture or creating new structures, as cleaning patterns or practices may be affected or power points may be obscured.

Suggestions for action

Each class can elect to adopt a particular corridor. This will depend on the lay-out of the school, and areas such as the entrance hall, lobby, assembly hall or dining room can be on a shared rota. It may be advisable to start with the corridors and move on to the cloakrooms and larger public areas only when the first improvements have been successfully established. Where pupil behaviour has been a problem, care should be taken to start with ideas which can realistically be controlled by regular usage.

Use the corridor walls at child-touch level for a variety of trails. These can be designed by the children and attached to panels mounted on battens. Include tactile trails with a variety of textures and shapes and word trails for all levels of ability.

Make the entrance hall welcoming with plants and displays. If there isn't enough room for these, an interesting notice board can establish a friendly atmosphere. Many schools have variations on a 'Welcome' board with, for example, the name of the school in clay letters, children's drawings of themselves at work and play, and of different members of the teaching and support staff, up-to-date photographs celebrating recent events and the progress of the playground improvement scheme.

Encourage the children to be responsible for selecting and mounting exhibitions of work, setting high standards of presentation and trying out various display techniques. Criteria established in discussion might include
— Is it interesting, self-explanatory, well written and accurate?
— Does it set a good example for younger children?

Split long corridors into short sections by design features. Long wide corridors which invite speed, noise and draughts can be made more interesting by island bays of seating, displays or plants. Techniques such as using different colours in each corridor section, regularly changing

Jane Launchbury

A 'WELCOME' BOARD IN A SMALL ENTRANCE HALL

themes for exhibitions, murals and mosaics, varying textures such as fabric or carpeting on walls, all humanise these areas and make them more enjoyable.

Construct display islands for larger objects in wide corridors, consider exhibition lighting. This need not cost much, as DIY parents, local shopkeepers or factories may be replacing fittings or have spare materials. Local timber yards can also be persuaded to donate free off-cuts. Where there is enough room, shelving can be used to break up long corridors and provide islands of interest. Pupils can be involved in the design, construction and erection of the shelves but remember Health and Safety regulations, possible fire hazards, LEA regulations and approval from the governing body.

Plan participation exhibitions. Children can be encouraged to try an experiment, play musical instruments, listen to music or solve problems. Different 'participation' themes can be chosen by each class in turn. These might be simple such as contributing to an exhibition of 'found art', stones or things of one colour, or involve solving problems, such as building an arch or creating a pulley using a selection of blocks and string.

'HANDS-ON' DISPLAY IN A CORRIDOR

Widen children's experience of adult art. Many municipal art galleries will lend prints and original paintings and change them each term. Schools in some areas join together to buy pictures for which they then have a rotating loan scheme. The museum service may lend objects, statues or pottery for display. Some schools keep a particular part of the corridor for these changing displays. Spotlighting them and playing tapes of appropriate music can make the experience more rewarding.

Link cloakroom tidiness to a whole school plan to improve the quality of the environment. This may well be more successful than constant exhortations to tidiness. The children themselves can suggest ways to improve the situation and will probably be able to devise ingenious ways to store problem items such as wellington boots and PE kit.

Behavioural change resulting from altering the physical environment is shown in the work of Roger Cole of Bishop Grosseteste College.

He has tackled vandalism in a number of schools by creating displays of material, initially in corridors, stairwells, cloakrooms and other common space. The materials on show have to be cheap and easily replaceable, but interesting to look at or to handle. They are intended to attract attention and, by their physical presence, to slow down the movement of pupils along corridors. Corridor changes have included pieces of carpet and upholstered armchairs. In the early stages the display material was stolen or broken and furniture was damaged, but by continually replacing these items, the incidence of damage began to fall so that, after three weeks, pupils could be given responsibility to maintain and update the displays. Teachers noted changes in pupils waiting in corridors during breaks and before lessons, the noise level fell and vandalism was reduced. In one school the displays have been highlighted by the addition of spotlights and the headteacher was so impressed with the improvement in both the appearance of the school and the behaviour of pupils that he arranged for more display space to be created by re-siting cloakroom pegs.

Roger Cole describes this approach as transferring model primary school ideas into secondary schools. The idea could make a valuable contribution to schools wishing to tackle their own litter, vandalism and graffiti problems through attitude-changing processes.

Resources

Art, Craft and Design in the Primary School
Edited by John Lancaster
National Society for
Education in Art and Design,
7a High Street
Corsham
Wiltshire SN13 0ES   Tel. (0249) 714825

The Mural Kit
Directory for Social Change, 1980, £2.50 inc. p&p
9 Mansfield Place
London NW3

How Not to Paint a Mural
Town Teacher Ltd   50p
25 Queen Street
Quayside
Newcastle upon Tyne, NE1 3DQ   Tel. 329541

Low Tech
Rick Ball and Paul Cox. Century £6.95.
Making furniture and storage units from waste.

Pictures without paint
20 slides illustrating the versatility of collage using
'recycled' scrap materials, £7.90 + VAT
The Slide Centre Ltd
Ilton
Ilminster
Somerset, TA19 9HS

The Thames and Hudson Manual of Mosaic
by J Mellentin Haswell, 1973.
All the information needed to create mosaics and how
to convert bottles into safe glass tesserae.

3.1.3 Staffrooms

For a variety of obvious reasons, staffrooms are often not the most inviting of places. Teachers, busy all day in their classrooms and around the school, rarely spend more than a few minutes at a time in the staffroom, using it mainly as a place for arrival and departure and frequently as a cloakroom and kitchen as well. It is difficult for an individual teacher to impose a personal view of order and comfort on a communal area for which no one feels directly responsible, but with group consent the staffroom can be made into a more congenial place to meet colleagues. Such improvement is also consistent with the pupils' efforts to improve their classrooms and the general school surroundings, and ensures that teachers are seen to be as concerned about the environment as their pupils.

Headteachers' rooms seem to range from comfortable sitting rooms with books, flowers, pictures, soft lights, curtains and carefully mounted children's work, to grim, uncarpeted places with empty bookshelves and two hard chairs for visitors. As it is from the head's study that potential pupils and their parents receive first impressions of the school and hidden messages about the head's attitudes and style of leadership, it seems important that this room should reflect a school policy of valuing and caring for the environment in which pupils spend so much of their time.

While a great deal depends on the physical structure itself and on its state of repair and decoration, much can still be done to make the staffroom and headteacher's room look attractive. Books, children's work, pictures, plants and flowers, comfortable chairs, curtains and cushions, a rug or carpet, cups instead of mugs - all make visitors feel at home and reduce the austere institutional feeling which makes human contact difficult.

Regrouping furniture, screening off the washing-up area in the staffroom (if space allows), removing out-of-date papers from the notice board, storing LA documents in ring binders, providing adequate pegs for hanging coats neatly, keeping the TES and other journals on a coffee table - all these are in themselves minor items, but collectively can make for greatly improved surroundings.

3.1.4 Growing things

Growing things can encourage a lifetime interest in gardening, horticulture and botany but, more immediately, plants and flowers soften hard surfaces and add life and colour to any building. Plants already flourish in the majority of primary school classrooms, but there are ways of making the most of these and of reducing the effort involved in their care.

Well designed containers made of appropriate materials are not only pleasant to look at, but retain moisture, resist frost and require minimum maintenance. Plants can be chosen which require little attention and yet give year-round pleasure. Planting medium, aspect and temperature conditions should all be taken into account and specialist advice on these matters would be helpful.

School entrances are often bare and uninviting. A tub of plants inside or outside the door, or if there is insufficient space, window boxes or hanging baskets, all help to remove the institutional atmosphere. One or two large plants are often more impressive and easier to clean around than several small ones, particularly in areas such as entrance halls with open spaces and high ceilings.

Suggestions for action

Ask the children to look at the growing things in the school and to make comments and suggestions for a co-ordinated school action plan. Hold a 'growing things' brainstorming session and ask for ideas for obtaining plants. These might include bringing cuttings from home, growing from seeds or pips, gifts from local nurseries, raising money to buy plants, etc.

Ask the local authority Parks and Gardens department for advice on the construction, siting and planting of tubs, hanging baskets and window boxes and on maintenance. They may also be able to give plants and cuttings, show the children how to take cuttings, prick out seedlings, etc. and advise on 'easy to grow' plants.

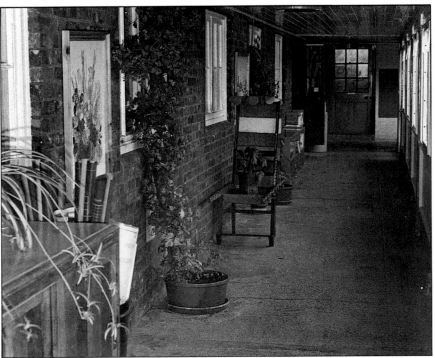

PLANTS AND PAINTINGS IN A CORRIDOR

Involve the PTA with the children in making various containers.

Make your own compost. Potting, cuttings and seed germinating media can be expensive, but the ingredients can be obtained cheaply or without cost.

A good general purpose compost consists of:
    1 part coarse sand
    1 part leafmould or well rotted compost or sedge peat
    2 parts rich topsoil (sieved through ⅜″ sieve)
    1 oz granular general purpose fertiliser ('Growmore')
    per bucketful of compost.

Grow as many plants as possible from seed. This is cheaper and far more exciting than buying seedlings. Experiment with different pre-treatments for seeds to see how these influence germination (this is cheapest with seed collected from native species, including trees). Try:

– soaking the seeds for 24 hours
– mixing the seed with damp sharp sand, tie in plastic bag
  and leave in a fridge for three weeks
– abrade the seed cases by rubbing with rough sandpaper.
  (Chip the tough cases of large seeds with a knife, but don't
  damage the growing point)
– combinations of the above.

Sow equal numbers of each seed type in small labelled pots. Cover with sifted compost as deep as the diameter of the seed. Water, and keep all pre-treatments under identical conditions. Record germination time and success rate for each treatment.

Propagation and growing-on seedlings in the classroom window can be difficult because of uneven lighting. To help remove this problem: Line a box (with the top and one side cut away) with cooking foil to reflect light on the seedlings or cuttings more evenly. At night cover the box with polythene to retain warmth and avoid draughts. Remove it in daylight to hasten warming by the sun. Many culinary herbs can satisfactorily be grown in the classroom.

Growing plants can be a good source of funds, selling well at bazaars and fêtes. Several are particularly suitable for this purpose, especially those which produce complete, easily potted, new growths such as spider plant *(Chlorophytum comosum vittatum)*, mother of thousands *(Saxifraga sarmentosa)*, devil's backbone *(Bryhophyllum daigremontianum)* and mother fern *(Asplenium bulbiferum)*.

Try the system below to overcome the problem of watering plants in the school holidays. This will avoid the need to arrange watering visits or rely on the school caretaker (who may be on holiday anyway).

Try establishing bottle gardens. They have the advantage of needing little attention during holidays and illustrate virtually closed systems

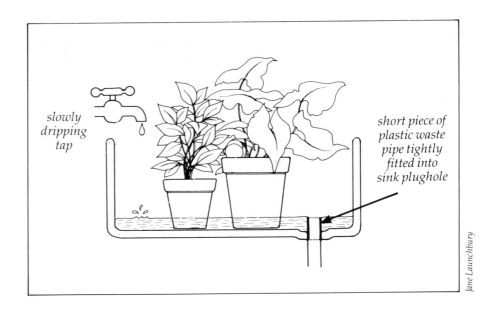

slowly dripping tap

short piece of plastic waste pipe tightly fitted into sink plughole

Jane Launchbury

in which water and nutrients are recycled whilst sunlight and air are the only inputs. Slow-growing plants needing a humid atmosphere are best - try ferns and mosses. Setting-up requires a few homemade tools and some advice, especially for narrow-necked carboys. See Resources 3.1.4.

Resources

Local authority Parks and Gardens Department
Local nurserymen and garden centres.

Bottle Gardens and Fern Cases
by Anne Ashberry, Hodder & Stoughton, 1965.

Letts Grow House Plants
Letts Grow Plants in Window Boxes
by Kenneth Bechell, Charles Letts & Co Ltd

Indoor trees
by Jack Kramer, Darton, Longman and Todd.

The Pip Book
by Keith Mossman, Penguin 1977.
Growing familiar, and unusual, plants from avocados and peanuts to kumquats and kiwis, the seeds of which can often be salvaged from the rubbish bin.

Success with House Plants
Reader's Digest ISBN 0-89577-052-0. Everything you could need to know!

Houseplants
Thomas Rochford. Wisley Handbook 14. Price £1.15.
ISBN 0-9066-03-02-01
An excellent series. Other titles include 'Plants for Small Gardens',
'Plants for Shade', 'Water Gardens', 'Gardening in a small space'.
Prices range from £1.15 - £2.00.
The Royal Horticultural Society
Vincent Square
London SW1P 2PE
(Also available in many National Trust shops).

Nature Detection and Conservation
by Jean Mellanby, Carousel 1972.
Ideas for indoor gardens of mosses and moulds, terraniums,
windowsill, wildflower nurseries and more.

3.2 Outside

We have all experienced the bleak institutional feel of many school playgrounds - and perhaps felt grateful that we don't have to spend hours of our time there. But playgrounds need not be such barren deserts. With planning and effort they can provide interest and excitement, shelter and security as well as facilities for satisfying and varied play. Pupils will benefit enormously if the grounds are an integral part of the educational process, with both structured and informal learning taking place in an environment which provides stimulus, support, delight and aesthetic pleasure. See 2.3 for the influence of play on behaviour.

3.2.1 Initial Assessment

When planning changes it is as well to consider the grounds as a whole, even if the initial proposals will be small. An overall view will help to ensure that early changes and developments do not conflict with others in subsequent years. An outline plan, on the lines of a structure plan for a region, or a development plan for a town, will be of great value.

Suggestions for action

Observe the children playing and see how they use available space. Is there bullying or roughness? Do certain groups dominate? Are there some groups or individuals that don't seem to play or relate at all? Which are the most popular places, games and activities? Are some places avoided?

Talk to the children, dinner supervisors, ancillary staff and school neighbours as well as parents and teachers, you may learn some surprising things about what happens at playtime.

Consider the needs that can be satisfied by well designed school grounds. Observe the children at play and see what is missing. The ideal might include opportunities for:
- exercise and the practice of varied physical skills and games
- imaginative and creative play
- enjoyment, rest, relaxation and privacy

- experience of well designed, cared for and aesthetically
  pleasing surroundings
- taking responsibility for changing a place and experiencing
  a sense of ownership
- caring for the place and its plants and animals
- enriching and supporting curriculum studies
- sharing with others in the school and wider community
- increasing contact between the school and the community.

Users of the school grounds may well have differing views of the relative value of retaining space for playtime football, competitive games and formal sports and providing opportunities for different sorts of play and learning experiences. Where space is limited this conflict will have to be resolved.

Work with a large scale plan, photograph or model of the school grounds and match proposals with locations. Various factors should be taken into account including wind directions, exposure/shelter, sunshine, access requirements for vehicles calling at the school, existing uses, possible services below ground, impact on neighbours, protection from vandalism and the need for undisturbed places. Particular criteria will need to be established for each item planned, for example ponds should be in relatively secure locations, sunny and not overhung by trees; tables and berry bushes for birds, flower beds and butterfly gardens should be easily observed from school windows; quiet areas should be in sunny or lightly shaded places; for maximum life painted murals should be on walls protected from driving rain and direct sunlight; woodland should not upset neighbours through shading or leaf fall.

Follow the planning proposals in 1.2 and involve the whole school community.

Discuss the options with the pupils. Keep the discussion general and let any ideas come forward - no matter how grandiose or apparently wild. Listing the ideas where everyone can see them will help generate more ideas. If pupils 'dry up', seed new ideas; many are outlined below. Avoid selecting one apparently good idea too soon without exploring other ideas adequately - it is best to give some time to raising ideas only without looking at them in detail.

Sections 3.2.2 and 3.2.3 examine further ideas for improving school grounds. For convenience they are listed under two headings: 'plant-related' and 'other physical features', but in reality they often overlap as shown in the case study on page 56. Other ideas for grounds can be found elsewhere, notably 4.1.

The plan and extracts from this article show that a difficult area such as a hard site can still provide a place for plants and a pool. Insect and bird study, plant types and textures as well as colour, light and shade and sound will all be enhanced.

'The best available space is a bare tarmac playground surrounded by buildings on all sides. There is no possibility of digging into the ground which is criss-crossed with pipes and cables. Interest is focused on raised features in corners and around the sides of the buildings, leaving the centre still free for formal play.

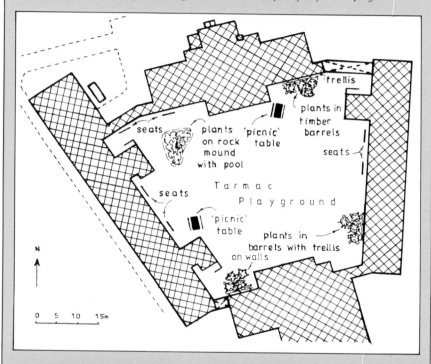

Advantage has been taken of sections of blank wall to hold trellis work for climbing plants. Timber materials are used throughout for the trellis, the seats and the half-barrel containers for the plants.

Groups of plants are cared for by different school classes. The children remove weeds, trim off dead growth, and spread fertilizer and mulch. They will add seedlings and plants which they grow themselves. They also have the opportunity to plant seeds of fast growing annuals, even sunflowers, and bulbs to flower in spring, summer or autumn.

The basic planting is a deliberate mixture of evergreen, golden and grey foliage shrubs with a variety of flowering types and berries. Some plants are smooth to touch, some velvety, and some have thorns. Scented plants and herbs add to the interest and to the uses which are made of these plants in classroom studies as well as out of doors.

The pool is placed on the mound at a height where the five year olds can (just) see into it from a 'viewing stone' at the edge of the mound. The pool creates its own micro-climate to add to the variety of temperature, humidity and other factors which can be experienced and measured around the playground.

The design and planning process is a vital part of the scheme. Children gain from researching into different aspects of the project such as investigations of local ecology and local wildlife habitats, and the study of the life cycle of individual plants and animals which they hope to see in their own special area. They have a lot of fun and learn a great deal from presenting to parents and school governors their hopes for the development of the special area. A presentation can take the form of essays and poems, drawings and measured surveys, and models.'

*Selecting an Area for Environmental Studies
by Patricia Green, Bulletin of Environmental Education,
November 1986.*

Resources

Learning through Landscapes

In September 1986 the DES, the Countryside Commission and Berkshire, Hampshire and Surrey County Councils launched a three year research project to
- *investigate the potential of the school grounds as a resource for learning and teaching*
- *investigate and design and management of school grounds*
- *report on the contribution that the design, management and use of the school grounds can make to improving environmental quality and educational opportunity.*

A project report is available for £3 from
Eileen Adams
Learning Through Landscapes Project
Third Floor
Technology House, Victoria Road
Winchester, Hampshire. SO23 7DG   Tel. (0962) 846258
A final report is due in 1989

Playground Design: outdoor environments for learning and development.

Aase Eriksen, Van Nostrand Reinhold, New York 1985.
Contains an excellent chapter on how to work with children to develop a better playground.

See also Resources 3.2.2 and 3.2.3.

3.2.2 Plant-related ideas
Suggestions for action

Create class areas for small experiments and activities.
These could include:
- the colonisation of bare ground
- the effects of cutting a 'meadow' area at different seasons
- growing vegetables and flowers
- soil profile pits and following a plant's root system
- a place to dig and handle soil.

These before and after photographs show the littered and compacted earth at the edge of the car park transformed into a colonisation experiment (foreground) and a hedgerow at Werneth Junior School, Oldham.

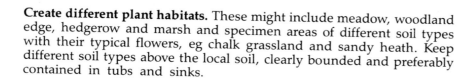

Create different plant habitats. These might include meadow, woodland edge, hedgerow and marsh and specimen areas of different soil types with their typical flowers, eg chalk grassland and sandy heath. Keep different soil types above the local soil, clearly bounded and preferably contained in tubs and sinks.

Plant
- a butterfly garden
- berry and seed-bearing shrubs and plants to attract birds in the winter
- a small area of coppice to produce roundwood for sale or use in the school
- a willow bed in a damp area, willow canes can be cut for basketwork.

A different class or year group can be responsible each season for the design and maintenance of flowerbeds on the main approach to the school.

Make a pond with a gradually shelving bottom for safety. Provide an adjacent concrete study area and edge with sleepers or telegraph poles for safety and seating. See Resources - for plastic linings. If natural clay is available this can be 'puddled' by the children to form a waterproof lining; this is cheap and can be effective, but it must not be allowed to dry out. The children can work with clay samples in the classroom to make watertight bowls and demonstrate the principle.

Creating a variety of habitats
Newtown Junior School, Newham Grange, Stockton on Tees.

Teachers, pupils and parents worked with Community Programme staff from the Tidy Britain Group to plan a native species woodland edge and meadow on the boundary of the school playing fields and a pond in the school quadrangle. Much of the heavy pond excavation was done by parents and TBG staff, but initial planning and subsequent lining and planting were done by the pupils. A chequer board garden and tree nursery are also planned.

COVERING THE POLYTHENE POND LINER

49

Make and run a tree nursery to grow collected seed. This could also provide material to extend planting beyond the school grounds.

Plant specimen trees - try several different native species.

The Forestry Commission or groups such as The Tree Council and Men of the Trees will often provide trees.

Community groups sometimes sponsor tree-planting. Local landowners often allow limited transplanting of tree seedlings from their land. Garden centres and nurseries selling trees and shrubs may give schools reasonable prices, but it is cheaper and more satisfying, if slower, to collect seed and establish a tree nursery.

Seeds of native wildflowers, grass/wildflower mixtures and trees can be gathered sparingly if the species are abundant.

Pupils from Seymour Road Primary School, Clayton, Manchester helping with a local authority tree-planting scheme (which also provided trees for the school grounds).

Build a compost heap. It provides an environment to study (worms, minibeasts, recycling, biodegradability) as well as nourishment for growing things.

Soften hard areas. Possible alternatives include: raised planting areas, plant troughs, old stoneware sinks, cast iron baths, hanging baskets and wall-climbing plants.

Greening a hard playspace at Byron First School, Bradford.

This school's yard was just asphalt running up to a 30' high buttressed retaining wall of plain brick. Tidy Britain Group MSC funded labour created the garden wall and the children planted two trees and spring flower bulbs.

Jane Launchbury

Resources

Pond building needs care and good materials. Plastic or rubber flexible liners are useful on a stable site. Black polythene (500 gauge) is cheapest but cannot be repaired and must be totally covered with sand or soil because it will deteriorate in sunlight. PVC liners can be repaired and are available with nylon reinforcement. Butyl sheeting is repairable and, like PVC, stretches to follow the shape of the excavation. Catalogues from Butyl Products Ltd and Visqueen Marketing Dept.

Butyl Products Ltd.
Radford Way
Billericay
Essex

Visqueen Marketing Dept.
Films Group
ICI Plastics
PO Box 6
Bessemer Road
Welwyn Garden City
Herts AL7 1HD

Conservation in School Grounds *(1987)*
British Trust for Conservation Volunteers
36 St Mary's Street
Wallingford
Oxon OX10 0EU   Tel. (0491) 39766

How to make a wildlife garden
Chris Baines, Hamish Hamilton, (1985) £8.95

Developing school landscapes as environmental resources: guidelines for schools
Planning Department
West Sussex County Council
Sussex House
Crane Street
Chichester,
West Sussex PO19 1RL   Tel. (0243) 777617

Nature by design
Hammond & King
Birmingham Urban Wildlife Group
11 Albert Road
Birmingham B4 9UA

Creating herb-rich swards
Wells, Bell & Frost
Nature Conservancy Council
Attingham Park
Shrewsbury, Salop

Making the Most of your School Grounds *(Parts 1 and 2)*
See Resources 2.1

Grounds for Conservation
See Resources 2.1

Nature from Nothing
Pauline Kaye, Cumbria Trust for Nature Conservation.
A useful pack offering guidance through all stages from surveys to management.
Cumbria Trust for Nature Conservation
Church Street
Ambleside
Cumbria LA22 0BU

Practical Nature Conservation
Nature in the Town
Resource lists for teachers from Council for Environmental Education, see Resources 2.1.

The Complete Urban Farmer
David Wickers, Julian Friedman Publishers
The definitive guide to producing crops in a small area.

Planning Your School Nature Garden
See Resources 2.1.

Cards to Plan Your School Nature Garden
£4.50 + p&p (send with order)
Urban Spaces Scheme. (Address in Resources 2.1)

Seed Bank
Stocks over eighty species of wildflower seeds.
44 Albion Hill
Sutton
Surrey SN2 5TF

John Chambers
Stocks a range of wildflower seeds.
15 Westleigh Road
Barton Seagrave
Kettering
Northants NN15 5AJ

W W Johnson & Son Ltd.
Stocks four wildflower mixes for use with grasses.
Stells Lane
Boston
Lincs
PL21 8AP

Grounds for Learning
A valuable pack covering development from initial surveys through planning, design and implementation. Useful advice on grants, materials and further help, plus some 'ecological games'.
Lothian Urban Wildlife Group
The Technical Block
Broughton Primary School
Broughton Road
Edinburgh EH7 4LD

Advice from:
Urban Wildlife Groups
County Wildlife Trusts
BTCV Regional offices
See Appendix 2.

3.2.3. Other physical features
Suggestions for action

Construct sheltered seating with tables for quiet play and reading. Try different materials and varied textures such as tree trunks and concrete. Top low walls or steps with rubber safety tiles for warmth, comfort and safety (the council playground officer will advise).

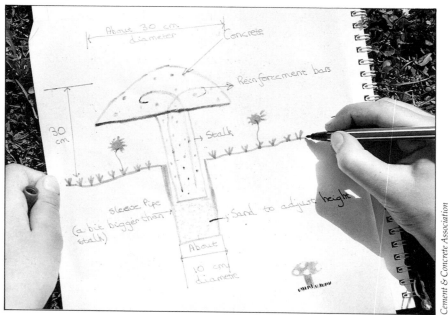

Cement & Concrete Association

DESIGNING CONCRETE TOADSTOOLS
(See Resources 3.2.3)

Cement & Concrete Association

MIXING CONCRETE FOR THE TOADSTOOLS

Use space between buildings or in suitable alcoves as an open air classroom. This can be roofed but open-sided, with permanent seating and tables of concrete or fixed timber and, if possible, a water supply. The room will offer potential for large scale beams, pulleys and levers study as well as waterflow, windmills and nature study. It will also make a useful bad weather play space.

Change the levels of the grounds. Heaps of rubble with a thin layer of soil, spoil from pond or structure foundation excavations or even road sweepings can all be used to increase available area, shorten sightlines and create interest where previously there was nothing to stop the eye. Different levels can be integrated in other plans for creating secret or sheltered quiet places, soil variations and adventure play spaces.

Try to provide as much variety as possible. There are endless possibilities including

- Games area with playground and walls marked out appropriately for hopscotch, skipping, ball games or chess and draughts.
- Sandpit and water play areas.
- Climbing, balancing, running and jumping structures, mounds or walls. Aim for a range of materials and use telegraph poles, tree trunks, railway sleepers, earth banks, tyres, concrete, bricks, stones and barrels.
- Murals, mosaics, sundial and sculptures with potential for regular changes in subsequent years. The theme of 'seasons' helps pupils to recall and visualise living features throughout the year and allows other seasonal factors to be illustrated, such as the sun's altitude and changes in the constellations.
- Paths which can make wild areas accessible all year. These can also be games (mazes in brick patterns and chase game routes) and nature trails.
- A space for outside demonstrations such as Morris dancing, sheep-shearing, and visits from ambulance personnel, refuse collectors or firemen.
- A place for bonfires, barbecues and outside cooking.
- Structures such as - a boat, gypsy caravan, play house or brick-topped banks for imaginative play.
- Facilities for community use such as sheltered seating for parents and toddlers to sit and relax while waiting for children; a garden for the disabled or elderly or BMX tracks for evening and holiday use.
- Secret places. These can take many forms, such as tunnels made from large pipes; thick shrubberies, tall fences, screens of trees or drystonewall. Some of these will also be of value to wildlife.

A SECRET PIPE EXIT FROM A RAISED SHRUBBERY
(Coombes County Infant School, Arborfield, Berkshire.)

The division between plant-related schemes and other features has been used for convenience. In practice they often come together as in this Plymouth example which came about when Pilgrim Primary School moved to a new building.

'Our Plan. Prior to our move we had made many plans as class projects, trying to include items pupils would like to see, apart from the oasis of manicured grass!*

From the outset we could see that the pupils required two different areas with a boundary between:
– a practical area where they would be able to grow flowers, vegetables, fruit and herbs,
– a wild conservation area where we could create a variety of habitats including a large study pool.

The boundary between these areas would be a series of low walls constructed of both natural and man-made materials, a geological rockery and three compost bins which could also be used as animal pens.

Funding. Such a project would require considerable funding and take several years to complete; from the start it was decided that the project was to be self-supporting. Pupils were to be involved in all stages of development even if they could not undertake all the physical construction. Consequently we had longer to collect funds but it did look as if the contractors were still on site three years after the school opened - the caretaker thought muddy footprints had come to stay!

We were fortunate in winning two prizes which helped us purchase pupil-size tools through County Supplies.

Apart from this, £425 was raised from the school raffle and tuck shop.

A Start is Made: Phase One. With tools and money a start could be made. Our plans were transferred on to the site with what seemed like hundreds of pegs and miles of string ready for the spade work.

First we started to lift turf from three junior gardening plots and the infants' chequerboard garden. All turf was cut, lifted and transported by the pupils; it was used to build a turf bank to the east of the site. Each plot was carefully trenched and dug over; builders' rubble and hundreds of granite pebbles were removed.

Materials. Phase One required paving slabs for construction of the chequerboard garden, timber for compost bins and concrete for the study pool. Our plans were sent to possible donors. Amalgamated Road Stone provided all the paving slabs, Tavistock Woodlands the timber and Pioneer Concrete all the concrete required for the study pool, free of charge.

Help! Contact was made with the Conservation Volunteers at the Plymouth Polytechnic and a group of five students joined us for one afternoon a week for a term. How enjoyable it was to see ten-year-old pupils working alongside young adults and parents. It was an afternoon which all the pupils looked forward to.

Progress is Made. Once all the plots had been dug, one area was laid with paving slabs alternating with soil. This was the infants' chequerboard garden - quite an exercise in problem-solving for the juniors working out the total number of slabs required.

Soon we could celebrate. Mrs Knott, our cook, baked a chequerboard cake - enough for everyone in the school. Each class was given several packets of seed to make a start on the gardening.

Study Pool. Within days of completing the garden plots a JCB was working noisily on an adjacent site excavating inspection trenches. We had previously checked with the Architect's Department that no services crossed the site of the proposed pool and we had stripped off all the turf. We were so pleased when the driver of the digger exchanged an hour's work for a school lunch - we had an instant pool!

Demolition of nearby houses provided us with rubble to grade the sides of the pool. Over 100 pupil-sized barrow-loads were shifted. Reinforcing mesh was donated by a local scrapyard and old packing cases acted as shuttering around the perimeter.

All the concrete, 6 metres^3, was provided free of charge. Early one Saturday morning parents, friends and pupils all helped, using hired tools, to move the ready-mix. Two hours later our pool was complete.

Bog Area. It was proposed to trap all overflow water from the pool in the adjacent bog area. Into a timber frame which was lined with polythene we unloaded forty used "Grow Bags" purchased from a local nursery. A bale of newspaper had raised enough money to purchase all the materials.

Compost Bins. An important part of our vegetable area was to be compost-making but we aimed to construct bins which could be used for a variety of purposes including the keeping of rabbits and poultry. All the timber was supplied by Tavistock Woodlands. Pupils were responsible for the construction and erection of the bins. Two bins are now used for rabbits, the third for compost making. Pupils are encouraged to bring items to school which can be put into the bin. Regular visits are also made to local beaches for seaweed and the stable of the local brewery drays for manure. All waste from the school kitchen, gardens and even the school vacuum cleaner is put into the bin.

Wild Area. Within the wild area a start was made to create a variety of habitats. This area, prior to the construction of our new school, had been planted some ten years previously with a variety of vegetation to soften the hard outline of the terraced houses. As it already had an established flora and fauna cover this area was selected as the wild area.

Sacks, wooden boards, stone slabs and metal sheets have been placed in one area to provide mini-habitats where pupils can observe temperature changes and colouration. A drystone wall, piles of rocks and piles of rotting wood have been created. Nettles and buddleia have also been planted in one area to make a butterfly garden.

Phase Two: The Past 18 Months. Much time has been spent by all classes in observing our progress and setting up their own experiments or just exploring. Our vegetable plots have provided us with a good variety of produce including runner beans, broad beans, onions, potatoes, carrots, turnips and radishes. The fruit area provided rhubarb, red and black currants and gooseberries. We have also acquired a large selection of natural and man-made rocks which have been incorporated into geology study walls, paths and seating.'

Adapted from 'Down to Grass Roots'
by Keith Loze in **Humanities Resource,**
Vol 1, Summer 1987
Wheaton Publishers Ltd.

Resources

The Tidy Britain Group has established Community and Environmental Education Projects under the Manpower Services Commission funding. In 1985 these projects employed over 1,000 people based in many areas of the UK. Most of the projects have staff who are willing to assist in the planning of environmental improvement schemes; further details can be obtained from the Tidy Britain Group.

Building and landscaping materials such as hardcore, timber, bricks, stone and topsoil are often available free from demolition sites or from local authority departments such as Waste Disposal, Recreation and Amenities (sometimes Parks and Gardens), Estates and Highways. Road sweepers collect tonnes of earth, grit and leaves during the autumn which provide a useful free source of potentially rich soil for landscaping.

Local companies often provide free materials, particularly items such as broken paving slabs, demolition rubble or excavated earth, which are classed as waste or of little value.

Redundant telegraph poles make excellent steps, retaining walls and fences and safe boundaries for ponds and wetland areas. British Telecom can be persuaded to deliver these free.

Other likely sources of help, advice and materials include

Local Authority Departments: Playing Fields, Health and Safety, Planning, Landscape and Architects, Parks and Gardens, Highways and the County Ecologist.

Local: **Naturalist Trust**
British Trust for Conservation Volunteers
Community Service Volunteers
army or other HM Service garrison
nurserymen and garden centres
builders' merchants
demolition contractors
timber yards.

Shell Better Britain Campaign

See Resources 1.2.

Making Playgrounds

Lin Simonon
Community Service Volunteers Advisory Service
237 Pentonville Road
London N1 9NJ   Tel. 01-278 6601

Do-It-Yourself Playgrounds

P. Frieberg
Architectural Press

This is concrete

Free folder of activities and information
Cement and Concrete Association
Mr D. Creasey
Fulmer Grange
Fulmer
Slough SL2 4QS

Concrete Toadstools; Concrete Evidence; Concrete in the classroom at Northfields Upper School; Children and concrete;

Four free leaflets on using concrete in schools to make useful objects. From Cement & Concrete Association, address above.

Meanwhile Gardens

Jamie McCullough
£1 + 30p postage
Calouste Gulbenkian Foundation, 1975

The Mural Kit
How not to paint a Mural

See Resources 3.1.2.

CHAPTER 4:
Responsibility for the Environment

4.1 Caring for animals and protecting wildlife

For many children, school provides their first real experience of relating to the animal world.

> *'As well as demonstrating a number of useful scientific principles, animals can encourage a caring and responsible attitude in the pupils themselves. Learning to handle them and knowing how to feed and look after them are valuable lessons, and becoming sensitive to their needs and showing a responsibility for their welfare are an important part of keeping animals in schools. Moreover, the way in which teachers regard animals, and the respect, affection and care with which they handle them, have an important bearing on the way pupils will react to animals in the future.*
>
> *Conversely, an uncaring attitude and bad management which includes rough handling, poor diet, inadequate caging and unsatisfactory husbandry will lead to some children developing an insensitivity and lack of respect for animals. The RSPCA believes that it is better for a school not to keep animals at all if it cannot be certain that the highest standard of care will be maintained.'*

Coombes County Infant School

The RSPCA handbook **Small Mammals in Schools** from which the above extract is taken, gives general guidelines on responsible animal husbandry, the educational use of animals in school and detailed information on keeping the more common animals, such as rats, gerbils and guinea pigs, (see resources 4.1). Many local authorities have their own guidelines and these should be followed.

Some teachers find that children lose interest in traditional school pets, particularly nocturnal hamsters and prefer to keep small farm-animals instead. Hens, sheep, pigs and even bees have all been successfully kept in both infant and junior schools. This is only possible where outside experts and adequate facilities are readily available - farm-animals are even more demanding of time and resources than traditional school animals and are certainly more difficult to board out during weekends and holidays. Several local authorities have formed liaison schemes where children can build up a relationship with a particular farmer and in some cases 'adopt' an animal. There are other schemes involving individuals or organisations bringing animals into schools. These have been reviewed by the RSPCA in conjunction with the CEE. It is advisable to consult the RSPCA publication, **Visiting Animal Schemes: a guide to good practice for schools, local education authorities and V.A.S. operators**, before agreeing to borrow or adopt an animal.

The majority of pupils enjoy furry animals and pets, and are concerned for the welfare of whales, pandas and large and exotic animals. Worms, snakes, spiders and insects may have less obvious appeal and are rarely regarded with the same respect and affection. A wild and weedy patch in the school grounds, a pile of logs, a piece of carpet left on a patch of earth, all encourage wildlife which the children can observe and enjoy spontaneously. Here they can learn to handle these less appealing creatures with care, overcoming any initial fear or revulsion.

Thousands of wild and domestic animals and birds die each year as a result of thoughtlessly disposed waste such as tins, bottles, plastic can-holders, fishing-line and weights. This is an area of great concern to many children and one in which they can have some influence, by disposing of waste carefully themselves and encouraging their friends and families to do the same. (This idea is developed in **Our Environment**, see Appendix 1.)

Suggestions for action

Discuss human and animal needs and the specific needs of animals in the classroom. Consider the conditions in which school animals are kept and improve them if necessary so that they provide a good example for pupils to emulate at home. The science adviser, science centre or City Farm may be able to lend hens and incubators, and bee hives, while some local farmers may lend animals such as sheep or goats for a short time or allow regular visits and adoption schemes.

Ensure that worms, insects and other living things brought into the classroom as specimens are handled carefully. They should be returned to their natural habitat as soon as possible. Give children ample opportunities to observe these creatures and feel familiarity rather than revulsion.

Create habitats for wildlife in the school grounds. Ideas include
- bird tables and other feeding stations which can be seen from classroom windows. Some types can be fitted onto classroom windows for close observation
- bat and owl boxes; nesting boxes for small birds
- a pond for endangered species such as newts and toads
- piles of wood to shelter invertebrates and small mammals, amphibians and reptiles
- an area of the grounds left to grow wild - 'weeds' encourage a variety of birds and insects
- sacks or wool carpet (biodegradable, not plastic-backed) laid on an earth bank to make a heat and humidity trap. Voles may build runs and nests underneath the carpet, and insects and other wildlife will flourish and can be observed under supervision
- butterfly gardens.

Discuss responsible pet ownership.
- Many dog owners train their animals to walk at heel and sit until called, but allow them to foul pavements and grass in parks where children play. Dog toilets exist in some areas - discuss possible local siting and investigate local bye-laws
- Thousands of dogs are abandoned each year by owners who no longer want them. Pupils can influence family behaviour and see that unwanted pets are taken to animal rescue centres rather than left on the streets.

Whitchurch Primary School

Study the danger to wildlife of wrongly disposed waste and litter. Broken glass kills and maims animals; birds become entangled in discarded fishing-line or plastic can-holders; grazing animals ingest plastic bags; swans and wildfowl die from lead-poisoning after swallowing fishing weights and shotgun pellets.

Run a 'Protect Wildlife' campaign in school using stories, posters, pictures and tapes and an exhibition of dangerous litter. Organise a similar 'Look After Your Pets' campaign.

Discuss the needs of animals in zoos. Design a cage or enclosure for a specific animal. Suggest ways of improving the environmental conditions at a zoo visited. Discuss 'Why have zoos?'

Given space and commitment a range of animals can be kept in school, as this example from Coombes County Infant School, Arborfield, Berkshire, shows.

'Hens have been kept at the school for a number of years. They will eat kitchen scraps or cheap grain, and their only disadvantage is the need to arrange for their care during the holidays. The school is lucky in this respect to have a resident caretaker and family willing to undertake the task. Hens will lay, hatch and raise their own families, but they will, with equal aplomb, hatch and care for ducklings, an enterprise not usually successful in an incubator.

Bees have been kept in window observation hives, but here the skills of bee experts from outside the school are frequently needed.

Two sheep, brought in as orphan lambs, have successfully been raised to maturity, and having been mated at a nearby farm, are confidently expected to produce lambs in early spring, but as a project this has needed effort in providing housing, fencing, grazing and supplementary hay. We needed grazing areas for them and have fenced off three 'fieldettes' and seeded these with ley grass and clover and will plant with a succession of downland wild flowers. The paddocks will be grazed in rotation and we shall plan our grazing policy round the flowering of these plants. But if replacement lambs and sheared wool can be produced, a cycle of vital importance to human society will have been demonstrated with child participation.'

from **Come Outside** (see Resources 2.1)

Resources

Small Mammals in Schools
Visiting Animal Schemes - A guide to good practice £1
RSPCA Action Pack. Strays: unwanted dogs £2
'It's too late for Tessie' Video £6.99 or free loan to group members.
The story of an ill-treated pet dog.
Send s.a.e. for catalogue of other materials.
RSPCA
The Causeway
Horsham
West Sussex RH12 1HG   Tel. (0403) 64181

Wildlife in Towns
Chart £1.50
There is also a large range of pamphlets and booklets (about 30p each, send s.a.e. for price list and details). Topics include building nest boxes and feeding birds.
Royal Society for Nature Conservation
The Green
Nettleham
Lincoln LN2 2NR

Bird Studies Using School Grounds; Birds of Town and City *33p*
Two of several RSPB Project Guides
Royal Society for the Protection of Birds
Head of Education
The Lodge
Sandy, Beds SG19 2DL

Nest boxes
Flegg and Glue
British Trust for Ornithology
Beech Grove
Tring, Herts

Birds in the School Grounds; The Food Chain in a Pond; The Ecology of an Oak Tree; The House-fly; Spiders, Snails and Woodlice
Posters
Pictorial Charts Educational Trust
27 Kirchen Road
West Ealing, W13 0UD

Care for your Guinea Pig. Care for your Hamster. Care for your Gerbil. Care for your Rabbit
Collins/RSPCA pet care guides. Obtainable from the RSPCA or high street bookshops.

Manual of Exotic Pets
An excellent reference manual for vets and lay people alike.
Obtainable from
British Small Animals Veterinary Association
(BSAVA) Publications
5 St George's Terrace
Cheltenham GL50 3PT

Look Around the Town - First steps in Understanding the Urban Environment. Our Environment
Both have sections on dangerous litter (see Tidy Britain Group materials, Appendix 1).

Come Outside
Video tape (VHS), see Resources 2.1.

An Incubator in the Classroom
Ann Trotman.
This has been reissued in a second edition as one of the many resource booklets available from the NAEE. Information is given on how to set up an incubator; suppliers of eggs and equipment; details of the stages involved in successful hatching, and ideas for education themes which can be developed for different age groups. Price £1.95 including p&p from
National Association for Environmental Education
West Midlands College of Higher Education
Gorway
Walsall WS1 3BD   Tel. (0922) 31200

Bats - A Project Pack for Schools

A comprehensive activity and information pack. Fifteen illustrated sheets provide background material and suggestions for work based on the biology of bats and associated folklore. Instructions are given on how to construct a bat box and how to join in bat conservation by linking up with the Fauna & Flora Preservation Society. Pack costs £2.50 including p&p from
Stirchley Grange Environmental Interpretation Centre
Stirchley
Telford
Shropshire TF3 1DY   Tel. (0952) 590 936

Back Garden Wildlife Sanctuary Book

Ron Wilson, Penguin, (1981) £2.95

Gardening for Butterflies

Avon Wildlife Trust
209 Redland Road
Bristol
BS6 6YU

Really Useful Insect Pack

Watch. £4.50 incl. postage
Royal Society for Nature Conservation
The Green
Nettleham
Lincoln LN2 2NR

Creating and Maintaining a Garden to attract Butterflies

John Killingbeck, pub NAEE, send for publications list and prices
NAEE
West Midlands College of Higher Education
Gorway
Walsall
W. Midlands
WS1 3BD

How to make a Wildlife Garden

Chris Baines
See Resources 3.2.2.

4.2 Reducing pollution

The ideas in Section Three will have helped to make pupils aware of the quality of their surroundings and hopefully more concerned about the wider problems of pollution and their role in improving the situation. Many of the highly publicised sources of pollution such as acid rain or nuclear waste are beyond individual control and can be frightening in their magnitude. There are, however, other forms of pollution such as waste or noise which affect health and the quality of life, where children, working with their teachers and parents, can take action and have a direct and observable influence on their surroundings. Some of the ideas are applicable to both home and school, others only to the home but both provide a good opportunity for the school and the pupils to influence and change behaviour in the community. While children obviously can't reduce radiation levels they can learn that governments and institutions respond to public pressure. They can write letters on environmental issues which concern them to, for example, MPs, industrialists, water authorities and local authorities.

4.2.1. Litter

Litter is unsightly and often dangerous. Litter is indicative of an uncaring attitude or of negligence and disregard for the environment. Litter management takes time and money which could be used for other purposes. It is also one of the few forms of pollution where individuals and small groups can exercise a significant degree of control. Problems of litter must be solved before genuine environmental improvement can take place.

Suggestions for action

Raise the litter issue. Pupils who have started trying to improve the school environment may already have commented on litter in and around the school. If the subject has not previously arisen, try asking the pupils to list the things they like and don't like about the school and its surroundings. It is more than likely that litter will be on many of their lists of dislikes.

RUBBISH BIN SURVEY

Encourage objective observation of litter. Once the pupils have observed litter, they can be asked to think of ways to prevent it. They may want to carry out surveys of litter in and around the school, find out where it comes from and plan ways of control and prevention.

One of the most appropriate survey techniques for studying distribution of litter is to divide the school and its grounds into zones - using existing physical boundaries where possible - and collect and weigh all the litter in each zone. This should be a dry weather exercise. It can be further refined by sorting the separately-collected litter into types, ideally using categories which will help interpret its source and/or the role of the litterer (eg bus tickets might be a useful category if they are in the grounds facing a bus route and bus stop; cigarette packets and cigarette stubs will probably not be litter created by pupils, etc.).

Carry out attitude surveys. Pupils may want to explore further who drops litter, why, and where; and to observe behaviour and identify particularly bad areas. Attitude surveys can be useful tools in this work. These may be restricted to attitudes to litter or can be extended to include other matters affecting environmental quality. The surveys could be for

REFUSE COLLECTORS PAY A SPECIAL VISIT TO A SCHOOL

fellow pupils or include other groups such as teachers or members of the public passing by the school. The exact content of the survey should be arrived at through discussion with the class, and might include items such as

- Do the respondents ever litter?
- Are there acceptable forms of litter?
- Are there acceptable places to litter?
- Who do they think causes most litter?
- Where does litter come from - apart from pedestrians?
- Does the respondent ever pick up litter?
- Where does responsibility lie - with the manufacturer, the retailer, the purchaser, or the council for failing to provide bins?

Keep questionnaires short and simple and try to limit the answers to YES/NO or to controlled choice (eg always/sometimes/never). If they are too open-ended it can be difficult, if not impossible, to draw any valid or useful generalisations from them.

Resite litter-bins in school, install extra ones and put up posters and exhibitions. Resiting bins requires the co-operation of caretaker and cleaners. Additional bins can be designed and made by the pupils following a study of existing designs. The container can be made in wood, concrete or brick though for ease of emptying it is better to buy metal or plastic basket liners.

Use 'Look Around the Town - First Steps in Understanding the Urban Environment', or 'Our Environment' as the basis for projects on the environment. *See Tidy Britain Group Materials, Appendix 1.*

Encourage children to be aware of litter outside the school and of particularly well kept or badly littered areas. They could propose ways of improving the situation and write to the local authority with their suggestions.

Once the situation has been assessed, pupils can be asked for suggestions for reducing the litter problem and improving any particularly badly littered areas identified.

Resources

Look around the Town -
First Steps in Understanding the Urban Environment
Our Environment
Beating Litter
Litter, Waste Management and Recycling Slide Pack.
These materials support all the activities mentioned in 4.2. See Tidy Britain Group materials, Appendix 1.

Pollution
Black and white photo-pack, 10 large photographs plus notes on pollution including litter, noise and radio activity.
Pictorial Charts Educational Trust, see Resources 4.1.

4.2.2. Domestic waste.

Uncontrolled and wrongly disposed domestic waste is a major environmental blight in this country: it is costly to remove and can be dangerous. Reuse and recycling can turn waste into a valuable resource.

Suggestions for action

Dispose of litter correctly.

Make life easier and safer for refuse collectors at home and school by:

- keeping refuse in clean containers with well fitting lids
- wrapping unpleasant, damp or smelly refuse in newspaper
- leaving broken glass in an open container by the dustbin where it can be seen, or take it to a bottle bank
- reducing the amount of refuse by using bottle banks, can banks and by saving clean waste paper for paper recycling schemes
- putting food and vegetable waste on a compost heap.

Reuse and recycle as much as possible (see 4.3.)

Consider installing a compactor or incinerator at school. This will reduce the volume or amount of waste to be taken away. The pupils can investigate the cost effectiveness of this, a particularly appropriate activity for schools controlling their own budgets who have to pay for extra containers to be removed. Comparing costs need not be complex. The purchase cost of the compactor or incinerator should be divided by its estimated life (say 10 years for example) and be increased by annual service or parts costs. The equipment will produce a volume reduction which relates directly to a reduction in refuse container loads. Thus the savings of container-emptying charges can be compared directly with the cost of the proposed system. NB the incinerator may have pollution implications - plastics should not be burned.

Remember that many batteries contain the poisonous heavy metals mercury, cadmium and lead and are potential pollutants. Car batteries should be taken to a local garage; recycling other batteries is not yet economically viable or centrally organised. EEC regulations may eventually enforce safer disposal methods.

Make a study of refuse collection so that pupils become interested in and aware of all the issues involved. The methods of collection and disposal are constantly changing and differ widely across the country. Speakers from refuse collection and disposal authorities can be invited to explain the local system and other options.

Collection variations include:
- council-provided wheeled dustbins with hinged lids (continental style)
- council-provided traditional bins
- council-provided plastic refuse sacks
- no council provision
- collection from kerbside, householders to put out refuse
- free/charged collection of bulky household items.

Domestic disposal alternatives include landfill, incineration, incineration with energy recovery and composting. Various forms of treatment to remove secondary materials are also in use (eg recovery of ferrous metal by magnets, separate collection of newspapers and turning refuse into fuel pellets).

Pupils can find out about local council services available for the disposal of waste. Descriptive leaflets, outlining services available and location of facilities are usually available from the County Engineer's Department, County Hall. Facilities include civic amenity sites, sump oil disposal tanks, collection service for bulky refuse. The quantity of garden refuse and vehicles, refrigerators etc. which is dumped suggests that many people are unaware of available services. The pupils can see that their parents and the local community are informed.

Dead pets can pose a disposal problem. Contact a vet to discover the best local disposal option. The bodies of dogs and cats should not be buried in water catchment areas!

The history of refuse and refuse disposal (closely associated with sewage and sewage disposal), gives a very different perspective on history to 'wars, kings and grand buildings'!

Resources

Information about local services and facilities is available from local and county councils. Many local authorities have an information service for schools and will supply speakers on a variety of topics. The County Engineer's Department may be able to arrange visits, for example to a refuse depot, incinerator or civic amenity site. Contact with the local authority is easier if it has adopted the Tidy Britain Group Community Environment Programme; part of the CEP is a public education campaign, the authority will be geared up to service schools.

Look Around the Town -
First Steps in Understanding the Urban Environment
Our Environment
Science Units 1 - 5, *especially*
Waste Management and Resources
All provide valuable information on wastes by type and quantities, and the various disposal/recycling options. See Tidy Britain Group materials, Appendix 1.

Waste and Recycling

Teaching resources list from CEE, see Resources 2.1.

Resources - Waste

Chart (with notes on reverse) covers food, packaging, sewage and recycling. £1 from
World Wildlife Fund
Panda House
Weyside Park
Godalming
Surrey, GU7 1XR

Glass Recycling

Chart and booklet. Free from
Glass Manufacturers' Federation
19 Portland Place
London, W1N 4BH

Banking on Glass

Free loan film/video from
Viscom
Park Hall Road
Trading Estate
London, SE21 8EL

Save-a-Can

Offers leaflets, posters and other information on can manufacture and recycling. A video and extra
information is available if the scheme operates in your area. Headquarters at
Queen's House
Forbury Road
Reading, RG1 3JH

UK Reclamation Council

Can provide detailed documents on recycling as an industry. Separate documents on paper, textiles,
ferrous and non-ferrous metals.
UK Reclamation Council
16 High Street
Brampton
Huntingdon
Cambs PE18 8TU

London Waste Regulation Authority

Can provide an excellent booklet on landfill techniques.
Jeff Cooper
London Waste Regulation Authority (N174)
County Hall
London SE1 7PB   Tel. 01-633 2786

4.2.3. Noise
Suggestions for action

Discuss what is meant by noise as opposed to sound. (Pupils will probably decide that noise is too much sound in the wrong place.) Discussion on tolerable and intolerable levels of noise will reveal interesting differences of opinion, particularly if adult views are included.

Think of ways to reduce noise in the school and classroom. These might include fitting foam plastic strips (draught excluder) under desk lids and rubber tips on chair legs; regrouping furniture to minimise constricted movement; devices to stop door banging etc. Long bare corridors generate noise; corridor walls lined with shelves or with 'island' bays will reduce both speed and noise. See 3.1.2.

Consider screens of trees and shrubs to reduce traffic noise intrusion.

Think of ways to reduce noise levels at home. These might include obvious ideas such as being considerate about when and where to play radios, levels of TV noise in densely populated areas, avoiding using drills and noisy machinery in the late evening, restraining barking dogs, avoiding banging car doors and being aware that noisy games and shouting can disturb neighbours.

Topics might include airborne sound; soundproofing; sound transmission through solids and general investigations into sound as a physical phenomenon. If a sound level indicator is available (see Resources), noise-level maps can be drawn using isolines or shading and pupils can conduct sound surveys and make comparisons of perceived noise levels with measured levels.

Resources

Local council Environmental Health Officers will have sound meters for measuring noise levels and may provide a speaker and demonstration. The Environmental Health Officers can be contacted via the town hall.

Sound meters *may also be available on loan from teachers' centres or science and maths centres. A simple but versatile sound level indicator is available for £80 + VAT and carriage from Offord Microscopes. The same company can supply a booklet of simple experiments, surveys and investigations using the indicator, for 15p and a large s.a.e.*
Offord Microscopes
Ticehurst
Hurst Green
Etchingham
East Sussex, TN19 7QT

Noise Pollution
Teaching resource list from CEE, see Resources 2.1.

Our Environment
Contains a section on Noise. See Tidy Britain Group materials, Appendix 1.

Quiet Please
A six page leaflet outlining steps that can be taken to minimise noise, from the National Society for Clean Air, see Resources 4.2.4.

4.2.4. Air
Suggestions for action

Everyone can make a contribution to reducing acid rain by using electricity more sparingly. 80% of UK acid emissions come from coal-burning power stations.

Minimise the need for bonfires by composting. Burn only dry woody waste and avoid burning plastic or tyres. Logs and branches can be cut up for fuel or piled up in corners to provide a habitat for small mammals, reptiles, invertebrates and fungi.

Avoid using aerosols. Some aerosols can cause lung and skin irritation and those which contain CFC propellant reduce the protective ozone layer in the upper atmosphere. The containers are expensive, and remain hazardously pressurised even when empty. Nearly all products available in aerosols are also available in simpler packaging.

Run an anti-smoking campaign. Pupils can inform parents of the dangers of smoking and passive smoking and can encourage them to give up smoking. They can devise ways of preventing their peers from starting to smoke.

Resources

Air Pollution
List of teaching resources from CEE, (40p + s.a.e.), see Resources 2.1.

Air Pollution (9 - 11 years).
A set of air pollution fact sheets and experiments which can be photocopied to provide class sets.
£1 includes p&p. Other educational and information material available. Write for list and prices to
National Society for Clean Air
136 North Street
Brighton BN1 1RG   Tel. (0273) 26313

Our Environment
See Tidy Britain Group materials, Appendix 1.

Science at Work *or an old copy of*
Spons Directory of Formulae
Books on making cosmetics and household cleaners.

Health Education Council
Smoking and health materials.
98 New Oxford Street
London

ASH education pack
for £1.22 incl. p&p
Action on Smoking and Health
5 - 11 Mortimer Street
London W1N 7RH

Local health authority speaker
Many local authorities have community health workers who specialise in health education;
contact your town and county halls.

Friend of the Earth
Leaflets and more detailed information on aerosols and acid rain.
26 - 28 Underwood Street
London N1 7JQ   Tel. 01-490 1555

The Air Game
1984 £1.50 inc p&p. A board game on air pollution for 2 - 4 players of 11 - 13 years
Resources for Learning Development Unit
Bishop Road
Bishopstone
Bristol BS7 8LS

Acid Rain - who cares?
29 minute film (16mm) or video cassette. Free loan, 1983.
A Swedish boy tries to persuade his English friend to do something about acid rain.
From the
Swedish Environmental Protection Board
Swedish Embassy
11 Montague Place
London W1H 2AL

4.2.5. Water
Suggestions for action

Reduce pollution

- use non-polluting pest control such as dregs from home-brewed beer (dotted around in yoghurt pots and jam jars) for slugs
- use compost and manure instead of chemical fertilisers
- do not put sump oil, paint, unwanted medicines, or other chemicals into drains, ponds or streams
- use biodregradable detergent and reduce the amount of detergent used in the washing machine. It is generally as efficient to use less detergent than the manufacturer recommends
- keep rubbish out of ponds or streams.

Use less water. Overloaded sewage treatment works are a major source of water pollution in the UK. Reducing water consumption reduces pollution because less dirty water has to be treated and sewage plants can function more effectively.

The scale of water use is often difficult to grasp. The following data gives the average person's daily consumption of water in the UK.

– domestic water consumption	120
– industrial water consumption	160
– industrial private supplies	70
– power station cooling water (much coming from estuaries or the sea)	210
	560 litres

Ways to save water

- wash hands or vegetables in a bowl and not under a running tap (as far as hygiene allows)
- place a brick in the WC tank to reduce the amount of water needed for each flush (toilet flushing uses one third of all domestic water consumption)
- only heat as much water as is needed in the kettle
- take a shower instead of a bath
- collect rain-water for gardens
- use a bucket rather than a hose to wash the car
- replace old washers and faulty valves to stop fittings dripping.

Many larger schools have a metered water supply which can provide data for calculations of per child daily water consumption at school.

If water saving measures can be taken (notably a brick in the WC cistern) then the effect of the measures can be looked for in the consumption graphs.

The history of water supplies (from the Romans onwards) provides a fascinating study and gives a very different view of earlier times from the more conventional approach to history.

Other interesting projects include water shortage in the Third World, irrigation, artesian wells, etc.

Resources

Our Environment
Science Unit 5: Waste Management & Resources
(especially pupils' booklets)
See Tidy Britain Group Materials, Appendix 1.

Blueprint for a Green Planet
John Seymour and Herbert Girardet. Dorling Kindersley.
Full of practical suggestions for putting pollution in its environmental context,
eg water pollution and the water cycle.

Water authorities
Contact via the phone book. Most will provide a range of booklets and posters; speakers can often be arranged, as can visits to sewage treatment and water treatment works.

DIY plumbing and central heating guides
These provide background information and diagrams of domestic plumbing systems.

Experiments on water pollution
By D Williams & D Anglesea, Wayland.
Contains many experiments (some needing chemical apparatus and simple chemicals) on water pollution.

Coprophilia or a peck of dirt
By Terence McLaughlin, Cassell 1971.
A comprehensive and compulsively readable account of the UK history of sanitation (water supply, sewage disposal and refuse disposal).

Water pollution
Information and resource sheets (30p + s.a.e. with order please) from CEE, see Resources 2.1.

Water
10 large monochrome photos plus notes on improvements in pollution control on the Thames, from Pictorial Charts Educational Trust, see Resources 4.1.

A Turn of the Tap
Free-loan film from
Guild Organisation
6 Royce Road
Peterborough, PE1 5YB

The River Must Live
Free-loan film or video cassette from
Shell Film Library
25 The Burroughs
Hendon
London, NW4 4AI.

4.3 Reuse, recycling and saving resources

Recycling or reuse reduces the rate of consumption of finite resources. It also reduces fuel consumption and consequent acid emissions and the wastes associated with processing raw materials.

Many of the ideas suggested in this section make excellent starting points for project work and are developed in **Our Environment.** Useful information will also be found in five science units, **Paper; Glass; Metals; Plastics** and **Waste Management & Resources,** especially the pupils' booklets. **Our Environment** and the **Science Units** are produced by the Tidy Britain Group, see Appendix 1.

The concept of reducing the wastes associated with processing raw materials is not an easy one. Many items of packaging perceived as waste or wasteful may contain alternatives to fresh produce which have, potentially, much greater quantities of waste in the form of, say, outer leaves, guts or feathers. INCPEN (see Resources 4.3) uses the example of frozen peas in a plastic bag vs. fresh peas in pods. The latter produces a considerable amount of waste for a flat-dweller, **but** can provide free soil conditioner and nutrients for a gardener.

The concept of resource conservation is also difficult for young children to understand because of the apparent absence of effects. Embarking on a *'Switch it off!'* campaign reduces acid emissions from power stations and while this effect is not immediately obvious, the reduction of electricity bills can be observed. No directly observable effect is apparent when, for example, buying goods in returnable bottles rather than using a bottle bank. Even more intangible are the benefits of not buying goods made of tropical hardwoods, where the potential environmental benefits occur many thousands of miles away. Because of these difficulties it is important to make the most of practical exercises to help pupils to appreciate the relationship between concrete and abstract ideas.

Suggestions for action

Make surveys of what is thrown away at home and at school and encourage suggestions for reducing, reusing and recycling wastes. If parents will co-operate, a chart can be put up next to each refuse receptacle in the home, a pencil hung next to it and each item recorded as it is thrown away. Further simplification can be made if the chart is turned into a list of items which can simply be ticked. It is important to ensure that the list contains comprehensive terms such as 'other paper'. This chart will give some idea of the enormous amount of potential resources which are thrown away each week.

Encourage discussion on resources and on wastes and decide what contribution can be made at the family and school level to resource conservation.

Contact the local waste collection authority and discuss the organisation of a recycling project in the school.

There are many opportunities both at home and school for recycling waste materials such as glass, tin-plated steel cans, aluminium cans and other non-ferrous metals, paper, cardboard and textiles.

All-aluminium carbonated drink cans can be easily recognised as they do not have side seams or separate bases and their sides are not attracted to a magnet.

It is essential to establish that there is a market for these items before beginning collection and to check regularly the continuation of the market and the price. The variable demand for secondary materials has significant and rapid effects on their value. It is also essential to ensure that there are adequate facilities for collection, transportation, baling or container-isation and storage.

Some scrap merchants take bags of crushed aluminium cans (and other non-ferrous metals). Rag merchants buy clean textiles, particularly cotton and wool, and old clothing in reasonable condition (mainly for export to Third World countries). Bottle banks are increasingly available and as there is no direct payment to the depositor they tend to remain available, unlike waste paper merchants who may refuse to accept paper if the demand falls. Some towns also have Save-a-Can skips.

Contact Oxfam, Guide Dogs for the Blind and other charities to find out what they are collecting. Items collected for sale might include stamps, aluminium foil and ring pulls.

Charities working in developing countries may also welcome spectacles, garden and other tools and some clothing.

Many towns have **Scrapstores** which can be charitable or voluntary bodies or projects funded with MSC money. These collect selected commercial and industrial waste and adapt it for use in play schemes and primary schools. If there is one near your school it offers a good way of demonstrating ways in which waste can be recycled and reused.

Find out if it is possible to collect newspapers and other grades of waste paper for recycling. There are two alternatives
- encourage the pupils and their families to contribute papers to an existing collecting scheme
- if storage is not a problem, the school can become a collecting point and sell paper to raise money for school funds. Make sure you have a merchant who will take the paper and be certain of the grade of paper he is willing to accept. He may only want newspaper and could reject a load if one bundle opened at random contained a magazine.

Encourage interest in the recycling of paper by making recycled paper and papier mâché objects in the classroom. Find out about commercial papermaking and the use of trees (see **Science Unit 1: Paper,** and **Paper: its history and uses**, Tidy Britain Group publications, Appendix 1).

Glass and Paper Recycling Projects with Keep Richmond Tidy

'The Borough of Richmond has a forward looking policy on waste and recycling. In conjunction with 'Keep Richmond Tidy', it arranges for participating schools to have a bottle bank or newspaper collection skip for a week. The arrival of the container is the culmination of one or two weeks of curriculum studies in which local authority and Keep Richmond Tidy staff work with teachers to present information and activities relating to waste, litter and recycling. This starts with an assembly and film show and goes on, in individual classes, to the use of TBG teaching packs.

PARENTS AND PUPILS WAIT TO USE THE SCHOOL'S OWN BOTTLE BANK

Parents are involved and save glass or paper at home until the arrival of the skip. Even bringing the waste into school becomes a learning activity as pupils monitor the waste glass or paper collected by quantity, colour and type.

Richmond offers cash prizes for the top three schools in terms of quantity per pupil collected in the week.'

Peter Mansfield, Recycling Officer
London Borough of Richmond on Thames

Encourage the pupils to consider repairing, giving to charity shops and jumble sales, and swapping (comics and magazines) as alternatives to throwing items away.

Where appropriate use kitchen waste to make compost.

Use returnable containers in preference to non-returnable ones. The energy savings are potentially substantial - see **Science Unit 2: Glass,** Tidy Britain Group publications, Appendix 1.

Encourage energy savings. There is a direct relationship between turning off lights at home or school and the emission of acid rain from mainly coal-burning power stations. Long-life, low energy consumption fluorescent light bulbs can be used to replace ordinary incandescent bulbs and thus save energy: the high initial outlay is outweighed by savings in running costs.

Find out about alternative energy. Solar energy and passive energy-saving features are becoming more common in the construction of buildings. Passive energy features include siting large windows to face south and small windows to face north, using conservatories to increase solar gain, extra insulation, double glazing and draughtproofing.

Find out and inform parents about draughtproofing and insulation. MSC funded projects provide insulation for elderly and disadvantaged people. Local authority grants are available for certain home insulation projects.

Encourage interest in healthy eating. Choose fresh foods and avoid colouring, preservatives and too much sugar and salt. Find out about nutrition and the composition (and packaging) of junk food.

Look at advertising and packaging and the ways in which they encourage consumption and influence diet.

Encourage a wish and a will to share resources. The pupils could forgo snacks at breaks and between meals and donate the money saved to a 'Live Aid' type of appeal. Publicity on local radio could spread the idea - how about one day a week across the LEA?

Pupils in an Avon primary school see concern for others come to fruition as paper, books and other supplies are loaded onto a lorry on the first leg of their journey to the Sudan.

Resources

Science Unit 1: Paper
Science Unit 2: Glass
Paper: its history and uses
Science Unit 5: Waste Management and Resources.

Unit 5 gives useful information on electricity production and associated environmental impact. Includes simple practicals illustrating the effects of acid rain and energy conservation through insulation and cookery techniques. See Tidy Britain Group materials, Appendix 1.

Some **local authorities** employ a **recycling officer**, usually based in the Technical Services, Engineer's or Waste Disposal departments.

Details of **local authority grant schemes** for loft insulation can be obtained via the town hall.

Save-a-Can   )
Glass Manufacturers' Federation)   *see 4.2.2. for details of these and*
The Reclamation Association   )   *other resources on recycling*

Scrapstores

Contact:
Federation of Resources Centres
Grumpy House
Vaughan Street
West Gorton
Manchester M12 5DU   Tel. 061-223 9730

The London Recycling Forum

A loose affiliation of London boroughs and voluntary groups, provides recycling information for London, which may also be useful elsewhere. A video on recycling in London is also available.
Contact:
Jeff Cooper
London Waste Regulation Authority (N174)
County Hall
London SE1 7PB   Tel. 01-633 2786

Guide Dogs for the Blind Association

Often collect saleable aluminium through local groups. Find your local group by writing to the association at:

ENGLAND   *Alexandra House*
and   *9 Park Street*
WALES   *Windsor*
         Berks SL4 1JR

SCOTLAND   *104 West Campbell Street*
         Glasgow G2 4TY

Waste Watch

Gives advice to voluntary groups who are interested in starting recycling projects and has a range of educational aids on recycling including a video called 'Why Waste' available for £6.
National Council for Voluntary Organisations
26 Bedford Square
London WC1B 3HU   Tel. 01-636 4066

Industry Committee on Packaging and the Environment (INCPEN)

For information on the industry view of food packaging, eg **The Benefits of Packaging** *and* **Packaging saves Energy:**
INCPEN
Premier House
10 Greycoat Place
London SW1P 1SB   Tel. 01-222 8866

Too Good to Waste *and* **The Wastefuls - Save their Energy** *(videos)*
catalogue from
Viscom
Park Hall Road Trading Estate
London SE21 8EL

Set of **four free charts:**
Switch off unwanted lights.
Turn down radiators.
Close doors
Close windows.

and **two free packs** *for primary pupils:*
Primary Energy Trails
Practical Energy Projects
from
Dept of Energy
Information Division
Thames House South
Millbank
London SW1P 4QJ

Children and Energy: Keeping Warm
A pack of activity cards, booklets and teacher's notes available on loan from the seventy BP Preview Centres or purchase at £2.75.
British Petroleum Education Service
PO Box 5
Wetherby
W Yorks LS23 7EH

Wrapping up. Time for energy *two free loan VHS cassettes from Shell Film Library, see Resources 4.2.5. for address.*
The Saving Game
A pack of cards and instructions for the different games to play,
free from
British Gas
PO Box 46
Hounslow
Middx TW4 6NF

Energy without End
by Michael Flood
Friends of the Earth, £3.30 inc. p&p. A well illustrated, brief, up-to-date overview of renewable energy, see Resources 4.2.4. for address.

Many education authorities and teacher training departments are developing resources or approaches on world education or development education which can be used to put our way of life in its international setting.

4.4 Adopting a piece of land

Adopting a piece of land can improve its appearance, increase the amount of space available for recreation and enjoyment and provide an extra resource for curriculum studies. It can also be a complex process involving long-term commitment and a great deal of time and effort. Careful planning and the support of the LEA, PTA, children, teachers and local community are all essential. See the Shell Better Britain Campaign guide in Resources 1.2.

Litchard Junior School

Choice of land

The most obvious piece of land to choose is one adjacent to the school which can be used as an extension of the school grounds. The first thing to do is to trace the owner of the land. You will be most likely to be given permission if the land belongs to a private landowner who already has a good relationship with the school or if it belongs to the council or is awaiting a development date some years ahead.

Involving the school and local community

Adopting land offers a unique opportunity to involve pupils, teachers and interested members of the local community in the process of design and planning and in seeing results take place over a period of time.

It is helpful to:

- Invite teachers to consider any proposed adoption in terms of their own curriculum needs, however utopian, and to make proposals based on these needs.
- Ask each class to offer one or more alternative plans arrived at over a period of discussion and consultation. This could well take a whole term or longer. See 'Planning a project', 1.2.
- Ensure that each class and governors, parents, councillors and interested local people are represented on a steering committee which make decisions and oversees progress.

The process of examining the site, judging its potential, planning resource needs and a timetable are all outlined in section 1.2, 'Planning a project'. The varied nature of off-school sites makes generalisations difficult, there are many useful resources available to help the determined.

Long term success is most likely when the whole community is interested and informed and contributes to the project.

Adopting derelict land adjacent to the school at Waterloo County Primary School, Blackpool.

'Land at the side of Waterloo Primary School has been a mess for years. The rutted tarmac gradually became an illegal tip for lazy locals.

Now, a transformation is under way. And the benefits will be greater than purely visual.

A voluntary scheme involving the Tidy Britain Group, the Lancashire Trust for Nature Conservation, Lancashire County Council, the MSC and - most important - the youngsters themselves, took off on the site this week.

The land, bought 40 years ago with plans to build a school kitchen and dining room on it, has never been used by the authority. Instead, rubbish and rubble have been dumped on it by unauthorised folk leaving broken glass, rusty wires and bricks.

"It has become a hazard and a disgrace", says headteacher Mr Harry Pilkington.

Ever since he came to the school six years ago he has campaigned for a clean-up. Now at last it's happening, and with the help of the school's willing 500 pupils, it could revolutionise life at Waterloo.

A new fence is to go up, provided by the county council, which will keep out the "fly tippers". A paved study area where youngsters can draw and work on hot summer days will be surrounded by lawns, a shrubbery, a wild nature area, a pond for environmental studies, and a neat and tidy car park.

The children themselves are helping to plan what is planted, and it will be a special project in the summer term for the second year juniors to cherish it and watch it spring to life.

The philosophy behind the work, which, it's hoped, will be backed by labour funded by the MSC, is to teach tomorrow's adults about conservation, recycling and a general anti-litter, anti-pollution consciousness.

Says Mr Derek Soulsby, education supervisor for the Tidy Britain Group, "The children are the important factor. You can't teach the older generation much about it, they're apathetic and expect someone else like the local council to clear away the litter. But you can get younger people involved - people who will take their new way of thinking forward into the future."

It may take six months, a year, even two or three, but with time, a green and pleasant area will appear. And the value to one school and the spin-offs to society in general could be immeasurable.'

From the Blackpool Evening Gazette

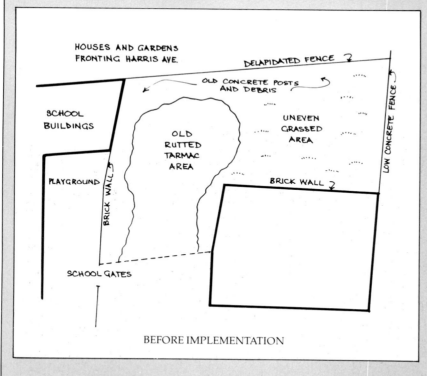

BEFORE IMPLEMENTATION

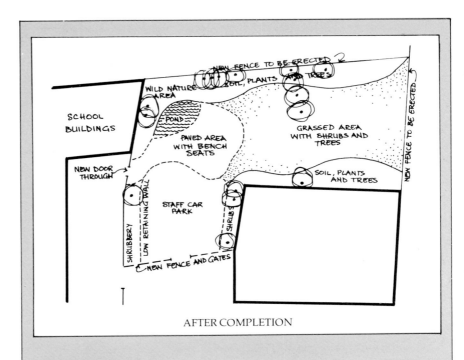

AFTER COMPLETION

MSC TEAM CARRYING OUT THE HEAVY WORK

Resources

See also 3.2.

Council experts

The process of adopting a piece of land is complex and may require negotiations with the owners and the drawing up of a licence. Rates may be incurred unless the authority rules that the use is not rateable. The local council can provide advice on tracing owners, obtaining planning permission, the rating position, ecological value of the site, location of underground services, sources of landscape materials, assistance with waste removal, possible financial help, etc. They can also provide speakers to help maintain interest and enthusiasm during the inevitable periods of delay.

Shell Better Britain Campaign Guide

See Resources 1.2.

Nature by Design

Birmingham Urban Wildlife Group   See Resources 3.2.2.

New Life for Old Space

Lists many other resources useful for schools planning to become seriously involved in adopting a piece of land.
Trust for Urban Ecology
Southbank House
Black Prince Road
London SE1

Promoting Nature in Cities and Towns: a practical guide

by Malcolm Emery
Trust for Urban Ecology, address as above
Croom Helm (1986) ISBN 0 7099 0970 5, £9.95 (400 pages). The first book to bring together all aspects of creating city nature parks - from reasons why - through how to start up - to creating habitat and management.

Waking up Dormant Land

£3.50 including p&p. Describes successful, and some not so successful, schemes from around the UK. From CEE, see Resources 2.1 for address.

British Trust for Conservation Volunteers

Schools affiliated to the BTCV can obtain advice, tools and insurance. In addition the BTCV administers the Queen's Silver Jubilee Grants Scheme which may be a source of funds for a project.
BTCV
36 St Mary's Street
Wallingford
Oxfordshire

Trust House Forte/Conservation Foundation

Grant scheme
11a West Halkin Street
London SW1 9JL

Parish Maps Project

A project designed to interpret the immediate locality in non-cartographical maps.
Parish Maps Project
Common Ground
London Ecology Centre
45 Shelton Street
London WC2 9HJ   Tel. 01-379 3109

Community Landscapes

Diane Warburton (ed) 1986

£3 inc. p&p. Eighteen case studies from the Manchester area, guidelines on running a project and twelve detailed design sheets including food growing, murals and trellises, seating areas and urban woodlands.

BCB
PO Box 28
Dumfries
Scotland DG2 0NS   *Tel. (0387) 720755*

APPENDIX 1:
The Tidy Britain Group
and the Research Project

The Tidy Britain Group, grant-aided by the Department of the Environment, is responsible for increasing public consciousness and appreciation of the environment, particularly through the prevention of litter and improved waste management. The Group's People and Places Programme is a systematic method of improving the environment based on changing public attitudes and practices towards rubbish and waste.

The Schools Research Project

In 1973 a research project was set up at Brighton Polytechnic to find ways of increasing pupils' sense of personal responsibility for the environment. Educational materials produced by the project are an integral part of the People and Places Programme.

The project works closely with teachers, local authorities, the Department of Education and Science and the Department of the Environment, other polytechnics, universities, the Welsh office, the Scottish Office, industry and national environmental groups. With the help of working parties of teachers, pilot materials are produced and are tested in classrooms in England, Scotland and Wales before being revised and published.

The project team:

Cherry Mares MPhil CertEd	Robert Stephenson BSc PGCE	Maisie Redhead
Project Director	Research Fellow	Project Secretary

Polytechnic Consultant: Professor Brian Hill DPhil BA FIL CertEd

Materials so far published include:

* Look Around: An Environmental Project Pack for 4-7 year olds.

Look Around is a valuable resource for any infant teacher planning a topic on the local environment. It is full of exciting and stimulating activities based on the school and its neighbourhood. Designed to develop children's knowledge and skills, the project also increases their awareness and appreciation of the environment and their sense of personal responsibility for it.

Look Around supports the National Curriculum and was tested in the classroom by practising infant teachers. It is relevant to the early years of education in Scotland and Northern Ireland and is also available in Welsh.

* **Our Environment** (7 - 11 years)

The second stage of the education programme and the basis for inter-disciplinary project work on litter and related problems in the local environment with the emphasis on science and language. Children start by studying the litter problem in the school and find out how it affects their local environment: they consider why problems such as litter, graffiti and vandalism exist and suggest how these could be avoided. Further assignments include work on packaging, recycling and refuse disposal, environmental quality, waste and pollution.

Produced by the TBG project team   £38.99 + VAT
and published by Thos Nelson & Sons Ltd
Nelson House
Mayfield Road
Walton-on-Thames
Surrey KT12 5PL

* **Litter, Waste Management and Recycling** (7 and over)

*A set of 40 slides with teacher's notes designed to complement **Our Environment**, but also useful in its own right. Topics include street cleaning, waste management, refuse collection and disposal, dangerous litter, water and sewage.*

£8.45 plus p&p

* **Beating Litter** (all ages: Teacher's Handbook)

A guide to reducing litter, graffiti and vandalism in schools. Suggests ways of increasing pupils' involvement in running the school and encouraging them to have more positive attitudes towards the school and its environment.

£2 plus p&p

* **School Links International**
   (Primary: Teacher's Handbook)

Based on a two year feasibility study with schools in Avon and around the world, this handbook gives suggestions for teachers involved in curriculum-related linking. It explains how pupils exchange information about themselves, their families, the places where they live and ways in which they care for and try to improve their environment. The aim is to give pupils a deeper understanding of themselves and their environment and to develop caring and responsible attitudes for the local and global environment.

Written by Rex Beddis, Senior Adviser Humanities, Avon County Council, and Cherry Mares, Director, TBG Schools Research Project.

£5.95 plus p&p

* Paper, Glass, Metals, Plastics, Wastes and Resources
(Key Stage 4)

Five science units which help pupils to understand the relevance of science in a technological society and to appreciate the environmental impact of that society. Pupils are encouraged to see how they can affect the quality of their environment in the decisions they make regarding the consumption, use and disposal of goods and services.

Price on application

* Paper: its History and Uses (11 - 16 years)

A video programme of interest to teachers of history and science and those concerned with environmental issues. It traces the growth of the paper industry with particular reference to the Industrial Revolution, the more recent diversification of uses for paper and paper products and the benefits of recycling. Complete with comprehensive notes.

£23.95 inc VAT

* Our Europe - Environmental Awareness and Language Development through School Exchanges
(11 - 16 years. Teacher's Handbook and worksheets)

Based on four years' pilot testing and development in the UK and France, 'Our Europe' shows how the traditional language exchange can be used to involve teachers of subjects right across the curriculum in environmental education. It provides suggestions for adding a new dimension to language exchanges.

£7 plus p&p

* There is also a series of occasional papers which describe the research involved in the production of these materials:

2 **Environmental Awareness** .... for the very young
3 **Environmental Awareness** .... through secondary science
4 **Environmental Awareness** .... through language exchanges
5 **School Links International - interim report on the evaluation of pupils' attitudes**

£1 plus p&p

All the above materials, with the exception of 'Our Environment' are available from:
    Tidy Britain Group
    The Pier
    Wigan
    WN3 4EX   Tel. (0942) 824620

The Tidy Britain Group Regional and National Offices are:

Keep Scotland Beautiful
Old County Chambers
Cathedral Square
Dunblane
FK15 0AQ

Keep Wales Tidy Campaign
1B Stangate House
Stanwell Road
Penarth
South Glamorgan CF6 2AE

Tidy Britain Group
83 Jesmond Road
Jesmond
Newcastle Upon Tyne
NE2 1NH

Tidy Britain Group
Astley Hall Cottage
Hall Gate
Chorley
PR7 1NP

Tidy Britain Group
Suite 5C
Josephs Well
Hanover Walk
Leeds LS3 1AB

Tidy Britain Group
The Chambers
28 St Edmunds Road
Northampton
NN1 5ET

Tidy Britain Group
Lion House
26 Muspole Street
Norwich NR3 1DJ

Tidy Britain Group
47 Oxford Street
Weston Super Mare
BS23 1TN

Tidy Britain Group
Premier House
12-13 Hatton Garden
London
EC1 2NH

Tidy Britain Group
4th Floor
Chandos House
26 North Street
Brighton BN1 1EB

Tidy Northern Ireland
123-127 York Street
Belfast
BT15 1AB

APPENDIX 2:
Local Conservation Contacts

County Wildlife and Conservation Trusts
(ED = Education Officer or team working with/for schools)

Avon Wildlife Trust (ED)
The Old Police Station
32 Jacob's Wells Road
Bristol BS8 1DR

Bedfordshire and Huntingdonshire
Wildlife Trust (ED)
Priory Country Park
Bakers Lane
Bedford MK41 9SH

Berkshire, Buckinghamshire and Oxfordshire
Naturalists' Trust (ED)
3 Church Cowley Road
Rose Hill
Oxford OX4 3JR

Birmingham Urban Wildlife Group (ED)
11 Albert Street
Birmingham B4 7UA

Brecknock Wildlife Trust
7 Lion Street
Brecon
Powys LD3 7AY

Cambridgeshire Wildlife Trust (ED p/t)
5 Fulbourn Manor
Manor Walk
Fulbourn
Cambridge CB1 5BN

Cheshire Nature Conservation Trust
(ED Wirral only)
Marbury Country Park
Northwich
Cheshire CW9 6AT

Cleveland Nature Conservation Trust
The Old Town Hall
Mandale Road
Thornaby
Stockton on Tees
Cleveland TS17 6AW

Cornwall Trust for Nature Conservation (ED)
Dairy Cottage
Trelissick
Feock
Truro
Cornwall TR3 6QL

Cumbria Trust for Nature Conservation (ED)
Church Street
Ambleside
Cumbria LA22 0BU

Derbyshire Wildlife Trust (ED p/t)
Elvaston Castle Country Park
Derby DE7 3EP

Devon Trust for Nature Conservation
35 New Bridge Street
Exeter
Devon EX3 4AH

Dorset Trust for Nature Conservation (ED)
39 Christchurch Road
Bournemouth
Dorset BH1 3NS

Durham County Conservation Trust
52 Old Elvet
Durham DH1 3HN

Essex Naturalists' Trust
Fingringhoe Wick Nature Reserve
Fingringhoe
Colchester
Essex CO5 7DN

Glamorgan Wildlife Trust (ED p/t)
Nature Centre
Fountain Road
Tondu
Mid-Glamorgan CF32 0EH

Gloucestershire Trust for Nature
Conservation (ED)
Church House
Standish
Stonehouse
Glos GL10 3EU

The Guernsey Society
c/o Le Chêne
Forest
Guernsey C.I.

Gwent Trust for Nature Conservation (ED)
16 White Swan Court
Church Street
Monmouth
Gwent NP5 3BR

Hampshire and Isle of Wight Naturalists'
Trust (ED p/t)
8 Market Place
Romsey
Hants SO5 8NB

Herefordshire Nature Trust
Community House
25 Castle Street
Hereford HR1 2NW

Hertfordshire and Middlesex Wildlife Trust
Grebe House
St Michael's Street
St Albans
Herts AL3 4SN

Kent Trust for Nature Conservation (ED)
The Annexe
1a Bower Mount Road
Maidstone
Kent ME16 8AX

Lancashire Trust for Nature Conservation
The Pavilion
Cuerden Park Wildlife Centre
Shady Lane
Bamber Bridge
Preston
Lancs PR5 6AU

Leicester and Rutland Trust for
Nature Conservation (ED)
1 West Street
Leicester LE1 6UU

Lincolnshire and South Humberside Trust
for Nature Conservation (ED)
The Manor House
Alford
Lincs LN13 9DL

London Wildlife Trust (ED)
80 York Way
London N1 9AG

Manx Nature Conservation Trust
c/o 14 Bowling Green Road
Castletown
Isle of Man

Montgomery Trust for Nature Conservation (ED)
8 Severn Square
Newtown
Powys SY16 2AG

Norfolk Naturalists' Trust (ED)
72 Cathedral Close
Norwich
Norfolk NR1 4DF

Northants Trust for Nature Conservation
Lings House
Billing Lings
Northampton NN3 4BE

Northumberland Wildlife Trust
Hancock Museum
Barras Bridge
Newcastle upon Tyne NE2 4PT

North Wales Naturalists' Trust (ED)
376 High Street
Bangor
Gwynedd LL57 1YE

Nottinghamshire Trust for Nature
Conservation (ED)
310 Sneinton Dale
Nottingham NG3 7DN

Radnorshire Wildlife Trust
1 Gwalia Annexe
Ithon Road
Llandrindod Wells
Powys LD1 6AS

Scottish Wildlife Trust (SWT) (ED)
25 Johnston Terrace
Edinburgh EH1 2NH

Shropshire Trust for Nature Conservation   (ED)
St George's Primary School
Frankwell
Shrewsbury
Shropshire SY3 8JP

Somerset Trust for Nature Conservation   (ED)
Fyne Court
Broomfield
Bridgwater
Somerset TA5 2EQ

Staffordshire Nature Conservation Trust
Coutts House
Sandon
Staffordshire ST18 0DN

Suffolk Trust for Nature Conservation   (ED)
Park Cottage
Saxmundham
Suffolk IP17 1DQ

Surrey Wildlife Trust   (ED)
'Hatchlands'
East Clandon
Guildford
Surrey GU4 7RT

Sussex Wildlife Trust   (ED)
Woods Mill
Shoreham Road
Henfield
West Sussex BN5 9SD

Ulster Trust for Nature Conservation   (ED)
Barnett's Cottage
Barnett Demesne
Malone Road
Belfast BT9 5PB

Warwickshire Nature Conservation Trust   (ED)
Montague Road
Warwick CV34 5LW

West Wales Trust for Nature Conservation   (ED)
7 Market Street
Haverfordwest
Dyfed SA61 1NF

Wiltshire Trust for Nature Conservation
19 High Street
Devizes
Wiltshire SN10 1AT

Worcestershire Nature Conservation Trust   (ED)
Hanbury Road
Droitwich
Worcestershire WR9 7DU

Yorkshire Wildlife Trust   (ED)
10 Toft Green
York YO1 1JT

Royal Society for Nature
Conservation (RSNC)   (ED)
The Green
Nettleham
Lincoln LN2 2NR   Tel. (0522) 752326

British Trust for Conservation Volunteers Regional Offices

East Anglia:
Animal House
Bayfordbury House
Bayfordbury Estate
Hertford SG13 8LD   Tel. (0992) 583067

East Midlands:
Old Village School
Chestnut Grove
Burton Joyce
Notts   Tel. (0602) 213316

London Ecology Centre
80 York Way
London N1 9AG   Tel. 01-278 4293

North East:
Springwell Conservation Centre
Springwell Road
Wrekenton
Gateshead NE9 7AD   Tel. 091-4820111

Northern Ireland:
The Pavilion
Cherryvale Park
Ravenhill Road
Belfast BT6 0BZ   Tel. (0232) 645169

North West:
40 Cannon Street
Preston
Lancs PR1 3NT   Tel. (0772) 50286

South:
'Hatchlands'
East Clandon
Guildford GU4 7RT   Tel. (0483) 223294

South West:
Newton Park Estate Yard
Newton St Loe
Bath
Avon BA2 9BR   Tel. (02217) 2856

Wales:
Forest Farm
Forest Farm Road
Whitchurch
Cardiff CF4 7JH Tel. (0222) 626660

West Midlands:
Conservation Centre
Firsby Road
Quinton
Birmingham B32 2QT   Tel. 021-4265588

Yorkshire and Humberside:
Conservation Volunteers' Centre
Balby Road
Doncaster DN4 0RH   Tel. (0302) 859522

Groundwork Trusts

These bring together many agencies to promote environmental action for the benefit of the local community. More are being created each year, but the following existed early in 1988.

Colne Valley Groundwork Trust
Denham Court Mansion
Village Road
Denham
Bucks UB9 5BG   Tel. (0895) 832662

East Durham Groundwork Trust
Unit 2a
Thornley Station Industrial Estate
Shotton Colliery
Co Durham DH6 2QA   Tel. (0429) 836533

Hertfordshire Groundwork Trust
Mill Green
Hatfield
Herts AL9 5PE   Tel. (07072) 60129

Macclesfield Groundwork Trust
The Adelphi Mill
Grimshaw Lane
Bollington
Macclesfield SK10 5JB   Tel. (0625) 72681

Merthyr Tydfil Groundwork Trust
Milbourne Chambers
Glebeland Street
Merthyr Tydfil
Mid-Glamorgan CF47 8AF   Tel. (0685) 73700

Oldham & Rochdale Groundwork Trust
8 Chapel Street
Shaw
Oldham OL2 8AJ   Tel. (0706) 842212

Rossendale Groundwork Trust
New Hall Hey Road
Rawtenstall
Rossendale
Lancs BB4 6HR   Tel. (0706) 211421

St Helen's & Knowsley Groundwork Trust
32 - 34 Claughton Street
St Helen's
Merseyside WR10 1SN   Tel. (0744) 39396

Salford & Trafford Groundwork Trust
6 Kansas Avenue
Weaste
Salford
Greater Manchester M5 2GL   Tel. (061) 848 0334

South Leeds Groundwork Trust
24 - 26 Great George Street
Leeds LS1 3DL   Tel. (0532) 462078

Wigan Groundwork Trust
Alder House
Alder Street
Atherton M29 9DT   Tel. (0942) 891116

West Cumbria Groundwork Trust
The Old Flour Mill
Cragg Road
Cleatamoor
Cumbria   Tel. (0946) 813088

UK City Farm Projects

Acorn Venture
Depot Road
Kirkby
Liverpool L33 3AR   Tel. 051-548 1524 (Site)

Ashford Community Farm
Kathryn Brooker
6 Northdown
Ashford
Kent TN24 8RB   Tel. (0233) 21711 (Home)

Balbirnie Community Farm
Balbirnie Park
Glenrothes KY7 6NR
Scotland   Tel. (0592) 752558 (Farm)

Beckton Meadows Community Smallholding
c/o 58 Buxton Road
Stratford
London E15 1QW   Tel. 01-519 2439 (Home)

Bill Quay Community Farm Associate
Hainingwood Terrace
Bill Quay
Gateshead NE10 0TL   Tel. 091-4385340 (Farm)

Bradford City Farm
Illingworth Fields
Walker Drive
Bradford BD8 9ES
West Yorkshire   Tel. (0274) 43500 (Farm)

Bulwell Urban Farm
51 Longclose Court
Crabtree Farm Estate
Bulwell
Nottingham NG6 8PZ   Tel. (0602) 765065 (Office)

Cardiff City Farm
Sloper Road
Grangetown
Cardiff CF1 8AB   Tel. (0222) 384360 (Farm)

City Farm Byker
Stepney Bank
Newcastle upon Tyne NE1 2PW
Tel. 091-232 3698 (Farm)

Clarence's Community Farm
Port Clarence Community Centre
Holly Terrace
High Clarence
Middlesbrough   Tel. (0642) 565614

Clayton City Farm
6 Foxdale Street
Clayton
Manchester   Tel. 061-223 2264 (Home)

Coventry City Farm
1 Clarence Street
Hillfields
Coventry CV1 4SS   Tel. (0203) 25323 (Farm)

Darnal Community Farm
Acres Hill Lane
Darnall
Sheffield S9 4LR   Tel. (0742) 441639 (Farm)

Dearne Valley Farm
c/o 1 Barnburgh Lane
Goldthorpe, nr. Rotherham
South Yorkshire S63 9PG   Tel. (0709) 897703

Deen City Farm
1 Batsworth Road
off Church Road
Mitcham
Surrey   Tel. 01-648 1461 (Farm)

Elm Farm
Gladstone Terrace
Lockington Road
Battersea
London SW8 3BA   Tel. 01-627 1130 (Farm)

Farset City Farm
638 Springfield Road
Belfast BT12 7DY
Northern Ireland   Tel. (0232) 231181 (Farm)

Freightliners Farm
Paradise Park
Sheringham Road
London E7   Tel. 01-609 0467

Friars Estate City Farm
105 Bradford Road
Idle
Bradford BD10 8SX   Tel. (0274) 616946 (Home)

Furness Improvement &
Development Organisation
c/o Furness Community Centre
Furness Avenue
Illingworth
Halifax
West Yorks   Tel. (0422) 248224 (Farm)

Glenand Youth & Community Workshop
Kennedy Way Industrial Estate
Blackstaff Road
Belfast 12
Northern Ireland   Tel. (0232) 618483 (Office)

Goat Farm
c/o The Lodge
Honeywood Walk
Carshalton
Surrey   Tel. 01-661 5500 (Work)

Gorgie City Farm
Gorgie Road
Edinburgh EH11 2LA   Tel. 031-337 4202 (Farm)

Gorse Hill City Farm
Anstey Lane
Beaumont Leys
Leicester LE4 0FL   Tel. (0533) 537582 (Farm)

Greater Possil City Farm
Ellesmere Street
Hamiltonhill
Glasgow G22 0PC
Scotland   Tel. 041-336 8754 (Farm)

Hackney City Farm
1a Goldsmiths Row
London E2 8QA   Tel. 01-729 6381 (Office)

Hartcliffe Community Park Farm
42 Briscoes Avenue
Hartcliffe
Bristol BS13 0LF   Tel. (0272) 784404 (Office)

Hawbush Urban Farm Association
c/o 17 Yorke Avenue
Hawbush
Brierley Hill
West Midlands   Tel. (0384) 262793 (Home)

Heeley City Farm
Richards Road
Heeley
Sheffield S2 3DT   Tel. (0742) 580482 (Farm)

Hockley Port City Farm
Hockley Port
All Saints Street
Birmingham
West Midlands   Tel. 021-551 6487 (Farm)

Holy Trinity Urban Farm
Holy Trinity School
Oakley Road
Small Heath
Birmingham B10 0AX   Tel. 021-772 0184 (Farm)

Huddersfield Community and
Heritage Farm
Peace Pit Lane
off Leeds Road
Deighton
Huddersfield HD2 1JE   Tel. (0484) 536239 (Farm)

Inverclyde Community Farm
c/o 47a Shankland Road
Greenock
Renfrewshire PA15 2QR   Tel. (0475) 42851 (Home)

Kentish Town City Farm
1 Cressfield Close
London NW5   Tel. 01-482 2861 (Farm)

Knowetop Community Farm
Castlehill Road
Castlehill
Dumbarton
Strathclyde G82 5AT   Tel. (0389) 32734 (Farm)

Lamont Farm Project
Barrhill Road
Erskine
Renfrewshire PA8 6BX   Tel. 041-812 5335 (Farm)

Lawrence Weston Community Farm
35 Barrowmead Drive
Lawrence Weston
Bristol BS11 0JH   Tel. (0272) 820276 (Home)

Liverpool 8 Garden Farm
c/o 34 Pilgrim Street
Liverpool 1   Tel. 051-709 4220 (Office)

Livingston Mill Farm
Millfield
Kirkton
Livingston
West Lothian   Tel. (0506) 414957 (Farm)

Meanwood Valley Urban Farm
Sugarwell Road
Meanwood
Leeds LS7 2QG   Tel. (0532) 629759 (Farm)

Millbrook City Farm
4 Church Lane
Highfield
Southampton   Tel. (0703) 555333 (Home)

Mudchute Community Farm
151 Manchester Road
Isle of Dogs
London E14   Tel. 01-515 5901

New Ark Adventure Playground
& Community Gardens
Hill Close
Reeves Way
Peterborough
Cambs PE1 5LZ   Tel. (0733) 40605 (Site)

New Park Adventure Playground
c/o New Parks Community Centre
St Oswalds Road
Leicester   Tel. (0533) 878239 (Site)

Old Rectory City Farm
The Old Rectory
Pear Tree Lane
Woughton on the Green
Milton Keynes
Bucks   Tel. (0908) 678514 (Farm)

Paper Mill Farm
186 Donnington Close
Church Hill
Redditch
Worcestershire B98 8QF   Tel. (0527) 67113 (Home)

People's Farm
108 - 122 Shackwell Road
Dalston
London E8   Tel. 01-806 5743 (Farm)

Rice Lane City Farm,
No 2 Lodge
Walton Park Cemetery
Rice Lane
Liverpool L9 1AW   Tel. 051-530 1066 (Farm)

Southwick Village Farm
271/273 Southwick Road
Sunderland
Tyne & Wear SR5 2AB   Tel. 091-548 9002 (Farm)

Spelthorne Farm Project
6 Burrows Hill Close
Heathrow Airport
Hounslow
Middlesex   Tel. (0753) 49330 (Home)

Spitalfields Farm
Thomas Buxton School
London E1   Tel. 01-247 1156

St Werburghs City Farm
Watercress Road
St Werburghs
Bristol BS2 9YJ   Tel. (0272) 428241 (Farm)

Stepping Stones Farm
Stepney Way
London E1   Tel. 01-790 8204

Stonebridge City Farm
Stonebridge Road
St Ann's
Nottingham NG3 2FR   Tel. (0602) 505113 (Farm)

Stour Valley
51 Honister Close
Quarry Bank
Brierley Hill
West Midlands DY5 1DL   Tel. (0384) 261518

Surrey Docks Farm
Commercial Docks Passage
off Gulliver Street
Rotherhithe
London SE16   Tel. 01-231 1010

Tam O'Shanter Urban Farm
Boundary Road
Birkenhead L43 7PD   Tel. 051-653 9332 (Site)

Thamesside Park Association
40 Thames Road
Barking
Essex IG11 0HH   Tel. 01-594 8449 (Farm)

Turner City Farm
c/o Turner Home
The Lodge
Dingle Lane
Liverpool L8 9RN   Tel. 051-727 8265 (Office)

Vauxhall City Farm
24 St Oswald's Place
London SE11 5LD   Tel. 01-582 4204 (Farm)

Walworth City Farm
Unit 5
Southwark Co-operative Development Agency
42 Braganza Street
London SE17 3RJ   Tel. 01-793 0526

Wellgate Community Farm
c/o St Marks Vicarage
187 Rose Lane
Marks Gate
Romford
Essex   Tel. 01-599 0415 (Home)

Windmill Hill City Farm
38a Doveton Street
Bedminster
Bristol BS3 4DU   Tel. (0272) 633252 (Farm)

Woodgate Valley City Farm Trust
c/o 12 Doulton Close
Harborne
Birmingham B32 2XF   Tel. 021-426 1871 (Home)

Wythenshawe Urban Farm
62 Langshaw Street
Old Trafford
Manchester M16 9LE   Tel. 061-437 3156 (Office)